Daily Vagus Nerve EXERCISES

Sally Roger

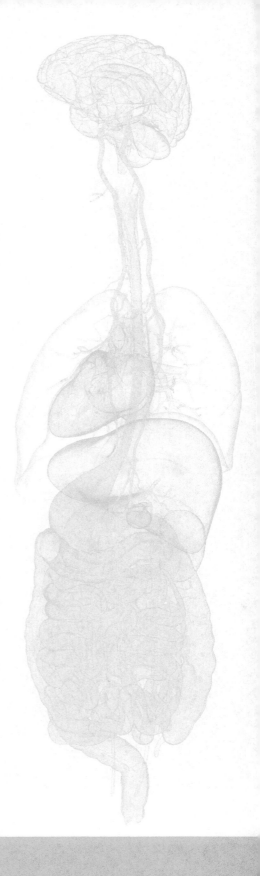

TABLE OF CONTENTS

CHAPTER #13: EIGHTEEN PRACTICAL STEPS TO STIMULATE NV NATIVELY

CHAPTER #14: 30-DAY MEAL PLAN **117**

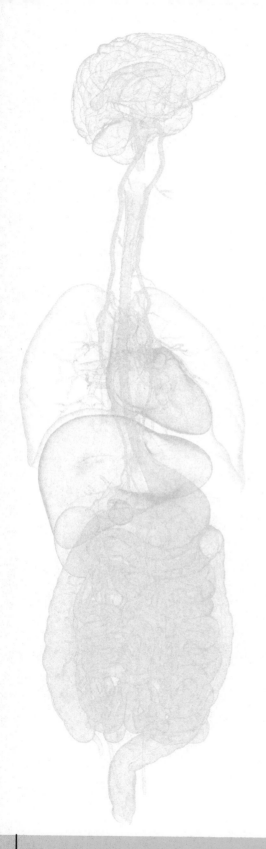

INTRODUCTION

The vagus nerve is found throughout our body and is in charge of the nervous system. It has many functions, including connecting the brain with organs such as the intestine, stomach, heart, and lungs. You are about to start reading a book that contains everything that refers to the vagus nerve. From its first chapters, you will know what it is, with complex concepts explained simply so you know what it is that you have in your body. You will know the anatomy and function of the vagus nerve and its relationship with the parasympathetic and nervous system with actions as elementary as eating without choking or increasing neuronal connectivity.

You will know why you should exercise your vagus nerve, what happens when you do not attend to it, and the advantages you can find when you take care of it and exercise. Then, it'll show you a wide variety of ways you can exercise it, from some that can take a while, like yoga sessions or breaths, to short 5 minutes to do on busy days or at the office. All made in such a simple way that you will not even have to move from your seat, just by breathing consciously or humming a song, you will already be stimulating the vagus nerve.

In addition to the exercises, you will know what you should introduce into your daily diet, with recipes and tips that you can include in it. At the end of this book, I include a 30-day program for the three main meals.

The exercises and tips I leave you in this book are backed by science. I will show you different studies for each one and the results so you can do each of them with total confidence. You can stimulate the vagus nerve and start feeling better from the first day.

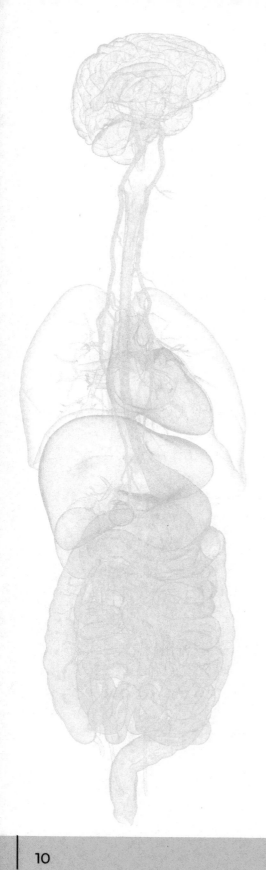

CHAPTER #1: WHAT IS THE VAGUS NERVE? | THE VAGUS NERVE EXPLAINED IN SIMPLE TERMS

The vagus nerve, or pneumoperitoneum, is the tenth of twelve pairs of cranial nerves. It originates in the medulla oblongata and innervates the pharynx, esophagus, larynx, trachea, bronchi, heart, stomach, pancreas, liver, and viscera, which are supplied by the superior mesenteric artery through the periarterial plexus to the myenteric plexus, or where the postsynaptic fibers are located.

It begins in petrous ganglion cells, which end at the level of the solitary tract in the medulla oblongata. It apparently originates between the accessory cranial nerve and the glossopharyngeal nerve in the posterior medullary sulcus or posterior olive grove.

It runs from the cells of the petrosal ganglion, then passes through the jugular foramen (posterior tear) at the base of the skull and into the postcolumnal space. This space connects the internal carotid artery and the internal jugular vein, which together form the main vascular-nervous package of the neck. Therefore, it descends the neck contained in this bundle on the posteromedial side of the sternocleidomastoid muscle (SCM). In its descent, it gives rise to the superior laryngeal nerve, which gives branches to the pharynx. Once in the chest cavity, the left and right vagus nerves behave differently:

Left Vagus Nerve

It enters the thoracic cavity between the left carotid and left subclavian arteries and gives rise to the left recurrent laryngeal nerve at the level of the aortic arch. It then travels down and forth (becoming anterior) and passes behind the pulmonary pedicle before reaching the esophagus, where it helps form the esophageal plexus.

Right Vagus Nerve

It crosses anteriorly to the right subclavian artery and, at this level, gives rise to the right recurrent laryngeal nerve. It then passes down and back (becomes posterior) and then down the back of the right pulmonary pedicle before it reaches the esophagus, where it also contributes to the esophageal plexus, as does its left pulmonary plexus.

In the chest cavity, the vagus nerve gives branches to the cardiac and pulmonary plexuses. Both vagus nerves pass through the chest cavity along with the esophagus, then enter the abdominal cavity and pass through the diaphragm through the esophageal hiatus. After entering the abdominal cavity, the left vagus nerve is distributed into the stomach, while the right vagus nerve ends at the solar plexus, from where it branches into the abdominal viscera (stomach, intestines, kidneys, and liver).

It is considered a mixed nerve with different afferents:

⊠ **Sensory afference.** Folds of the Eustachian tube, middle ear, and epiglottis.

⊠ **Parasympathetic afferent.** Heart, bronchi, and abdominal viscera.

⊠ **Ambiguous core afference.** Pharyngeal-style muscle (swallowing muscle).

The Most Important Branches

- Recurrent laryngeal
- Upper laryngeal
- Atrial branch (Arnold's nerve)
- Lower cervical branch
- Pharyngeal branch
- Heart branches
- Cardio-Thoracic Branches
- Esophageal plexus branches
- Pulmonary plexus branches
- Hering-Breuer reflex in the alveoli
- Anterior vagal trunk
- Posterior vagal trunk

The vagus nerve runs parallel to the internal jugular vein and the common carotid artery within the carotid sheath.

Cervical Branches

The lesser occipital or mastoid nerve rises and is distributed in the skin of the mastoid region.

- Nerve from the ear, ascending, to the skin of the pinna.
- Cervical cutaneous nerve, which runs laterally to the skin of the suprahyoid and subhyoid regions.
- The supraclavicular nerve descends and innervates the skin in the upper and outer parts of the chest.
- The supra-acromial nerve innervates the skin of the shoulder stump.

Functions

The vagus nerve sends parasympathetic motor fibers to each of the organs from the neck to the second transverse colon, except the adrenal glands.

- The stomach.
- The ear.
- The larynx.
- Back of the nose and throat.
- Amygdalin region.

The vagus also controls some skeletal muscles, including the following:

- Upper, middle, and lower pharyngeal constrictors.
- Cricothyroid muscle.
- Levator soft palate muscle.
- Palatopharyngeal muscle.
- Palatoglossal muscle.
- Salpgolpharyngeal muscle.
- Muscles of the larynx (speech).

This means that the vagus nerve is responsible for several tasks, such as gastrointestinal motility, heart rate, sweating, and many muscle movements in the mouth, including speech (through the recurrent laryngeal nerve). It also has afferent fibers that innervate the inner part of the outer ear where we listen through the ear branch, also known as Arnold's or Alderman's nerve and part of the meninges.

The fibers of the vagus nerve that innervate the pharynx and the back of the throat are responsible for the gag nerve. In addition, stimulating the vagus nerve of the bowel's 5-HT3 receptor-mediated afferents induced by gastroenteritis is one of the causes of vomiting. Cervical vagus nerve stimulation (e.g., during certain medical procedures) may cause vasovagal syncope.

The vagus nerve also plays a role in feeling full after you eat. It has been shown that if the vagal nerves are inactivated it can cause hyperphagia (substantial increase in food intake). It is also responsible for picking up sensations from the larynx and provides a motor component to the larynx through two branches: the recurrent laryngeal nerve (accessory nerve fibers) and the superior laryngeal nerve.

The Vagus Nerve and the Heart

The parasympathetic innervation of the heart is somewhat controlled by the vagus nerve and is shared with the thoracic ganglia. The vagus and spinal ganglion nerves mediate the slowing of the heart rate. The right vagus innervates the sinoatrial node. In healthy people, the parasympathetic tone of these sources closely resembles the sympathetic tone. Overstimulation of the parasympathetic nerves can promote bradycardia. When overstimulated, the left vagal branch predisposes the heart to an atrioventricular node block.

Here, neuroscientist Otto Loewi was able to prove that nerves secrete substances called neurotransmitters, which affect receptors in target tissues. In his experiments, Loewi electrically stimulated the vagus nerve in the frog's heart, which slowed the heart rate. He then removed the fluid from the heart and transferred it to the heart of a second frog without a vagus nerve. The second heart slowed down without electrical stimulation. Loewi described the substance released by the vagus nerve as Vagusstoff, which was later discovered to be acetylcholine. Drugs that inhibit muscarinic (anticholinergic) receptors, such as atropine and scopolamine, are called vagus nerve-blocking agents because they suppress vagus nerve activity in the heart, gastrointestinal tract, and other organs. Anticholinergic drugs, which are used to treat bradycardia, increase heart rate.

Physical and Emotional Effects

When the vagus nerve is activated excessively during emotional stress, the parasympathetic nerve is overcompensated by the strong response of the sympathetic nervous system that is related to stress. It can also generate vasovagal syncope because cardiac output suddenly falls, which can generate cerebral hypoperfusion. Vasovagal syncope usually affects young children and women more than other groups. It can also lead to temporary loss of bladder control during times of extreme fear.

Research has shown that women with complete spinal cord injuries can experience orgasm through the vagus nerve, which extends from the uterus and cervix to the brain.

Lesions of this nerve can occur in its branches, and if they occur in the pharyngeal branches, dysphagia can occur. On the laryngeal branch, paralysis of the cricothyroid muscle and weak voice can occur. Or if the recurrent laryngeal nerve also presents lesions: vocal cord paralysis, dysphonia, and hoarseness. Both laryngeal nerves can be affected, causing hoarseness.

Simple Explanation of the Vagus Nerve

The name of the vagus nerve originates from the Latin *nervus vagus*. Its root word means to wander, and the truth is that it describes the way it wanders through the body just as a tramp does. The vagus nerve is divided into two parts: one on the right side of the body and the other on the left side of the body. It begins in the brainstem approximately behind the ear, descends on each side of the neck, crosses the chest, and reaches the abdomen.

The vagus nerve connects the brainstem to almost every organ in the body, including the heart, lungs, stomach, intestines, pancreas, liver, kidneys, spleen, and gallbladder. It affects almost all vital organs. It's like a big, critical highway or transatlantic phone line with thousands of optical fibers on it, experts compare it. 80% of the wires are sensors, meaning that the entire vagus nerve tells the brain what's happening in every organ in the body.

In scientific terms, the vagus nerve is the main component of the parasympathetic nervous system, which controls our body's functions and involuntary behavior.

You have the sympathetic nervous system, which is part of the nervous system that initiates action, and the parasympathetic nervous system, which you can think of as its off switch.

So, the vagus nerve of the parasympathetic nervous system serves to change the body's patterns of rest, relaxation, recovery, heart rate regulation, and breathing—basically, all the fun things you need to live with.

So, experts note if the vagus nerve is the conduit that communicates with sensors that send signals from the body to the brain, this could directly impact our thoughts, thoughts, and even how we feel.

CHAPTER #2: ANATOMY AND FUNCTION OF THE VAGUS NERVE

Without thinking about it or making any special effort, today your heart will beat about 100,000 times, your lungs will breathe about 23,000 times, you will blink about 12,000 times, and your blood will pass through your body traveling through the body 3 times per minute; your liver is busy cleaning the same blood throughout the day. The bacteria that live in your gut are an ever-changing population that work with your digestive tract so it can absorb the nutrients your cells need to function and stay alive.

Did you ever wonder how all these things that are completely out of your control happen? How do complex and laborious processes happen together? The answer is in the autonomic nervous system, a true miracle of evolution. Our bodies are designed to live and survive without conscious thought. Imagine if every moment we had to tell our lungs to breathe or our heart to pump blood. Our evolution is closely linked to our ability to think consciously. If this was ever possible, it was partly because the systems necessary for survival became self-regulating.

The vagus nerve, as you know, the longest of all the nerves in the skull, has control over the parasympathetic nervous system and oversees, possibly, a number of critical health functions, transmitting sensory and motor impulses to every organ of our body. There are many complexities in this intricate and mysterious neural network.

It is a way of transmitting direct information about a person's state to the brain of the brain. It has great relevance for all diseases where mobility or movement is vitally important. The vagus nerve is one of the few nerves that start directly in the brain; that is, it does not occur in the spinal cord, nor are there other intermediate transfer stations. Its immediate boss is the brain. This is one of the things that explains the much-discussed connection between the gut and the brain today.

As for the function, we found that this nerve is responsible for bringing sensitivity to the entire ear area and outside the ear canal. It also detects taste and transmits proprioception to the mucous tissue of the larynx and pharynx, which acts to protect the airways. It also intervenes in the innervation of the muscles responsible for swallowing and vocalizing. Its main motor and sensory functions are the thoracoabdominal organs, namely the heart, intestines, blood vessels in the area, lungs, and carotid sinus.

Therefore, when the vagus nerve is affected due to all the tasks mentioned above, we find severe dysfunctions in the body since verbal communication, taste, heart, esophagus, larynx, and pharynx are altered by lack of motor innervation, sensitivity, and internal spontaneity.

The Relationship with the Parasympathetic and Nervous System

The parasympathetic nervous system is a branch of the nervous system that allows us to relax and recover from stress in our day-to-day routine. It serves to maintain tranquility, slow down our heart rate and our breathing rate so that we can breathe deeply and fully, divert blood from our extremities to our internal organs, make our body recover, stay calm, and even procreate.

A good part of the control of the parasympathetic nervous system is related to the vagus nerve. It regulates the control of the heart, lungs, neck, airway muscles, liver, stomach, kidneys, pancreas, spleen, gallbladder, small intestine, and parts of the large intestine, so the function of this nerve affects health decisively, and even then, remains a great unknown.

If this area is of interest for research, it is because of its length, structure, and thickness. It is relatively accessible if we compare it with other complex parts of the nervous system, such as since it could also be the brain, since there are indications that it could be the path to new treatments for certain conditions, such as migraines, chronic pain, or certain heart conditions.

Today, methods are tested to stimulate the vagus nerve to increase its activity, for example, to dilate blood vessels, to treat certain blood vessel disorders, or to control pain or relaxation. Certain normal functions of the vagus nerve are being tried to improve to help us develop treatments. I think this is an area that will grow, although it still needs some years of research and testing.

It Helps to Control Inflammation Levels

Just like computer wires, groups of neurons in our nerves send information through electrical signals that, after reaching nerve endings, trigger the release of chemical signals called neurotransmitters. These neurotransmitters bind to receptors on the cell receiving the signal and have an effect on the cell at the end of the connection.

The main neurotransmitter used by the vagus nerve is acetylcholine (ACh), which has a powerful anti-inflammatory effect on the body. Control of the inflammatory system is one of the most important functions of the vagus nerve. Common diseases associated with high levels of inflammation include Alzheimer's, arthritis, asthma, cancer, Crohn's disease, diabetes, coronary and cardiovascular disease, high blood pressure, or any disease that ends with the suffix inflammation.

It Allows Us to Eat Without Choking

When eating, we don't think about the process when we swallow something and stop the reflex from breathing so we don't choke. This important task is controlled by the vagus nerve. The pharyngeal branch of this nerve controls the five muscles of the pharynx. Also, it controls the active motor component of the gag reflex (which causes vomiting if something touches the back of the throat or the back of the tongue to prevent suffocation).

It Enables Speech and Relaxation

Did you know that it takes effort to keep your upper airway open with every breath you take? The muscles involved in this process are also involved in vocalization. If you've ever wondered which nerve allows you to communicate verbally with those around you, the answer is simple: the vagus nerve.

In the lungs, activation of the vagus nerve slows the breathing rate and makes breathing deeper. During the resting digestive phase, breathing tends to be deeper, coming from the diaphragm rather than the accessory muscles of the breath, and the respiratory rate tends to be lower. Slow, deep breathing activates the vagus nerve and stimulates the relaxation reflex as the person transitions from a fight-or-flight state to the rest-and-digest phase.

It Warns Us to Stop Eating

The feeling of satiety occurs when our brain receives signals from the vagus nerve. After eating, vague neurons send information to the brain about how much fat, especially triglycerides and linoleic acid, goes to the liver. This activates the function of the vagus nerve, which sends signals to the brain to create a feeling of fullness and the desire to stop eating.

An inactive vagus nerve may not be able to transmit this signal, which can lead to constant hunger, lack of satiety, and overeating at mealtimes. When the vagus nerve works efficiently, a person feels full in less than 15 to 20 minutes after a meal.

It Increases Neural Connectivity

Recent studies have shown that the presence of gut bacteria is essential for the development and maturation of the central nervous and enteric nervous systems. As we have seen, the vagus nerve is heavily involved in the transmission of information from the gut microbiome to the brain. This communication chain may be responsible for activating the production of a protein called "brain-derived neurotrophic factor." Activation of this factor leads to increased neural connectivity and, more importantly, to the generation of memories in the brain.

Other studies have shown that constant stress can negatively affect the normal function of the nervous system, especially the vagus nerve, so finding ways to relax seems crucial to maintaining good performance. In certain life situations, hypervigilance or stress can cause the vagus nerve to become unstable or dysregulated. This is important because we are talking about the Nerve of all systems.

Symptoms of Pathologies Related to the Vagus Nerve

It is not easy to discern whether the pathology is related to a pinch or another type of disorder of this nerve. However, some symptoms can catch our attention, such as the following:

- Difficulties when swallowing.
- Headaches.
- Insomnia or difficulties in bedtime.
- Thyroid problems.

- Irregular heartbeat.

How Are Vagus Nerve Pathologies Diagnosed?

The problem when making diagnoses about pathologies related to the vagus nerve is that the symptoms can be confused with symptoms that lead to other health problems.

Vagal Tone

Vagal tone is a measure of vagal activity used to assess the health of your autonomic nervous system. A healthy autonomic nervous system should be characterized by a high vagal tone. This means that the vagus nerve is very active and communicates with the body's organs.

Medical conditions and lifestyle factors impact the vagus nerve, which can reduce vagal tone. Methods to stimulate the vagus nerve may increase vagal tone and protect against certain psychiatric and inflammatory disorders. The vagus nerve is part of the parasympathetic nervous system. Parasympathetic innervation helps regulate body rest and digestive responses. Vagus nerve stimulation increases parasympathetic nerve activity, and parasympathetic nerve stimulation increases vagus nerve activity.

You can stimulate the parasympathetic and lazy nerves by practicing yoga, stretching, and meditation. Vagal massage can also help.

Available Methods to Stimulate the Vagus Nerve

I advance some available methods (Later, I will explain in detail and based on studies).

Vagus Nerve Massage and Massage Therapy

Vagal massage is a therapy that makes use of moderate pressure and vibrations near the neck to help with the vagus nerve, stimulating parasympathetic activity. The trapezius and sternocleidomastoid muscles are massaged along the sides and back of the neck to massage the vagus nerve that passes under them.

One study found that a 10-minute vagal massage significantly increased vagal activity and helped with relaxation. Shoulder massage with light pressure also helps with vagal activity and relaxation, perhaps by stimulating the entire parasympathetic nervous system.

General massage therapy is a great way to increase vagal tone. It broadly activates the parasympathetic nervous system and inadvertently triggers a vagal massage. The vagal benefits of massage therapy include increasing serotonin and dopamine, improving symptoms of depression and anxiety, improving focus, reducing chronic pain, and reducing cortisol levels.

Slow, Deep Breathing

Breathing at a slow pace, known as resonant rate, puts the autonomic nervous system in balance and helps with the ability to handle stress. This is achieved by increasing parasympathetic activity (rest and digestion) and decreasing sympathetic activity (fight or flight). The resonance frequency varies from four and a half to seven breaths per minute, depending on the person.

A 2017 study had participants complete 15 minutes of resonant rate breathing, followed by a stress test. They found that resonant frequency breathing can improve mood, increase vagus nerve activity, lower blood pressure, and dampen the stress response.

Yoga and Meditation

Meditation, stretching, and yoga are also effective tools for modulating the stress response by stimulating the vagus nerve.

One study got participants to achieve a guided meditation session of four hours per week for four weeks. Each station had a duration of two hours where stretches, breathing exercises, awareness of sensations, and feelings and gratitude exercises were done. The sessions resulted in significant vagal tone and lower anxiety levels compared to the control group.

A meta-analysis studied data from 17 randomized control trials that tested the effects of yoga on the autonomic nervous system. If you do 60 to 90 minutes of yoga per week, it is effective in reducing perceived stress and making a change to parasympathetic innervation. This means that the parasympathetic response is stronger than the sympathetic one, so the autonomic nervous system remains calm.

Stress Is Detrimental to the Proper Functioning of the Vagus Nerve

Some research points to meditation and breathing techniques as possible tools to consider in these situations. Yes, it helps, but you also have to keep in mind that in some cases, stimulation is more important. We are Mediterranean, and our vagus nerve lives where we already are. Adapted to this specific geographical environment, with a certain amount of energy, light, heat... Our genes also come from here. If you are a Buddhist and live in an elevated area, with little oxygen and not hot in Tibet, maybe this is the way to relax: breathing, meditation, mindfulness... But in my opinion, on the contrary, in the Mediterranean, we have enough energy, and we cannot control so much through mindfulness and breathing (although they also help), but most importantly, through exercise and movement.

Tibetans cannot be told to start running because they are drowning, starving for oxygen, and then having to learn other ways to relax on their own terms. I want to draw attention to this because it is clear that breathing and mindfulness help, but if we moved more, maybe we would not have to depend so much on these tricks, which is what is happening in the areas where we live.

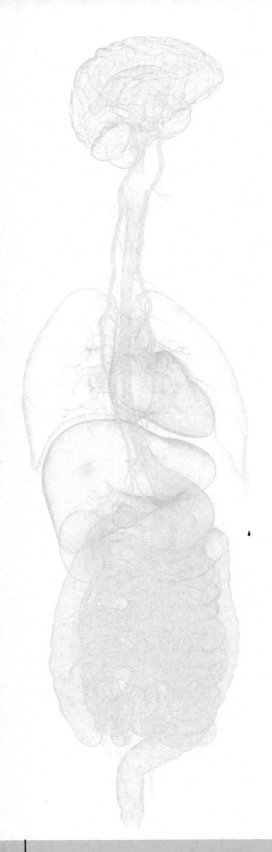

CHAPTER #3: WHY EXERCISE YOUR VAGUS NERVE?

The frenetic pace of today's society, added to everything that the changes of recent years mean, is generating problems of activation of the parasympathetic nervous system and deactivation of the sympathetic nervous system: fear, stress, anxiety, uncertainty... when the sympathetic nervous system is at the limit. Cortisol (the stress hormone) and adrenaline pump our bodies, and the vagus nerve tells the body that it needs to calm down, releasing hormones like oxytocin or proteins like prolactin to help calm us down. However, when this communication does not work fluently, chronic imbalances develop, leading to disease and dysfunction.

Over the past few years, the circumstances we have been through have created a space of ambiguity and uncertainty. There is a light at the end of the tunnel, but there is a feeling of tiredness and uncertainty. This can take the form of stress that affects our health. Right now, that's when we need our mental and physical strength the most, where cortisol skyrockets. A hormone that is not bad in itself is a survival hormone, which produces glucose when you need it and maintains blood pressure but is activated in our brain 24 hours a day, which ends up exhausted, inflamed, accelerating aging, and prone to diseases.

Constant cortisol affects our immunity and our neuroplasticity, the brain's ability to adapt to change and learn new things. Hence the importance to connect, stop, rest, digest, and send blood to a series of organs that, if not received in time and devoid, show signs of pathology. The digestive and reproductive systems will be the two biggest victims of the overactivation of the sympathetic nervous system and the abolition or inactivation of the vagus and parasympathetic nerves.

The parasympathetic nervous system has the role of recovery, tissue care, digestion, breathing, absorption, and rest. If you know how to activate it, you will have a very important endogenous tool in your body that has healing power. Here you can talk about the concept of "Health Reset," be able to listen to each of us and analyze what happens to each of us, know what happens to your digestion, and what happens to your breathing. Everyone can be a sculptor of their brain if they put their mind to it.

The longest nerve in the body has control and exchanges signals with everything from the mouth to the colon, and when it fails, the most common chronic diseases in humans occur.

When you think about being healthy, it immediately comes to mind what you eat, the exercise you do (or rather, the exercise you don't do), and the amount of alcohol or tobacco you consume. These are some of the determinants of our health and abilities from childhood to adulthood. However, discoveries in recent years have shown that the causes of many preventable diseases and ways to prevent them are linked to one nerve: the vagus nerve.

Through all these organs, the vagus nerve has the role of controlling the most important automatic vital processes, such as breathing, heart rate regulation, digestion, inflammation, and Rapid Eye Movement (REM) sleep. It also serves to regulate mood with the release of hormones associated with relaxation and stress reduction, such as serotonin, oxytocin, dopamine, and endorphins.

The main nerve of the well-known parasympathetic nervous system, the vagus nerve, is the "brake pedal" of our body that has the role of inducing the state of "digest and rest" that our cells need to regenerate. Signals through the vagus nerve go both ways. This means that messages passing through our heart, stomach, or lungs return to the brain via the vagus nerve.

The Vagus Nerve in Health and Disease

When it functions well, the vagus nerve plays an important role in our overall health and well-being, helping us to be relaxed during difficult times or stressful situations. However, when the vagus nerve is weak, it can cause many conditions, such as stomach problems, headaches, anxiety, fatigue, depression, or autoimmune diseases. Research suggests that poor vagal tone can cause an increased risk of heart attack or stroke because it affects heart rhythm regulation.

How do we know if our vagus nerve is normal? One measurement is called "vagal tone" and indicates the health, strength, and function of this nerve. Measuring electrical signals from our body's nerves is complex without surgery, but it can be approximated by measuring heart rate variability (HRV), a "substitute" for measuring heart rate. True vagal tone. While accuracy varies, HRV measurements can be obtained through certain heart rate straps, smartwatches like Apple Watch, and even some mobile apps that use a camera to measure heart rate, such as Welltory.

Heart rate variability is the variation between inhalation (where the heart naturally speeds up) and exhalation (where the heart naturally slows down). The difference between these two values indicates how strong the vagus nerve is. HRV values show our body's ability to move from an active state to a resting state. Athletes are known to have higher vagal tone, causing their heart rate to slow faster than others after exercise.

Experiments have been conducted with direct stimulation of the vagus nerve. For example, stimulating the branches leading to the heart reduces the heart rate. Some implants send signals to the vagus nerve to help prevent seizures in people with epilepsy. Other experiments have used vagus nerve stimulation to treat depression and addiction. Specifically, alcoholism. Women with spinal cord injuries can experience orgasm by stimulating the vagus nerve that runs from the uterus to the brain.

Having a strong vagus nerve also has its disadvantages. Some people activate the vagus nerve during emotionally stressful situations, causing what's known as "vasovagal syncope," a sudden drop in blood pressure and heart rate that causes dizziness and fainting. This is also the mechanism that causes temporary loss of bladder and sphincter control during times of extreme fear.

The Vagus Nerve and Chronic Diseases

According to a recent review of studies, due to its importance in the body, the vagus nerve has a key role in the development of chronic diseases: obesity, diabetes, heart disease, and possibly cancer. These diseases have three causes that, in turn, are controlled by the vagus nerve:

Oxidative Stress

This occurs when the body produces more oxidants than antioxidants, which can lead to DNA damage. Pollutants, tobacco, alcohol, and psychological stress can increase oxidative stress. Stimulating the vagus nerve has been found to reduce oxidative stress levels in the body.

Inflammation

This is what our body responds to that protects us from diseases, puts immune cells into action, and also to any sign of danger, whether by injury, a viral infection, or psychological stress.

Inflammation helps with the development of cancer and atherosclerosis, which helps with heart attacks. It also leads to insulin resistance, a factor that can trigger diabetes. The vagus nerve can reduce inflammation by acting on the Hypothalamic Pituitary Adrenal Axis (HPA) that controls the stress response and inhibits the production of inflammatory messenger cytokines.

The Stress Response

The overactivity of our sympathetic nervous system has been linked to cardiovascular disease, chronic obstructive pulmonary disease, and diabetes. The vagus nerve, a key nerve of the parasympathetic nervous system, is defined as responsible for reducing this activation and, among other things, increasing blood circulation, which protects against the disease.

In addition to the physiological factors of these diseases, the vagus nerve also influences the behaviors that lead to the disease. Risk factors such as smoking, junk food, or a sedentary lifestyle play a decisive role in the development of the disease. Well, the vagus nerve also affects these behaviors and lifestyles. Smokers are known to have lower HRV (i.e., vagal tone) and HRV drop can be measured after smoking. The vagus nerve can regulate the brain's executive functions, including emotional self-regulation, impulse suppression, memory, and problem-solving. In other words, a weak vagus nerve takes away your willpower to eat well or exercise.

The advantage is that you can strengthen it!

In summary, we can conclude that strengthening the vagus nerve will greatly improve our health, but how to strengthen the nerve? The answer is: similar to a muscle, use it. The first step is to measure our vagal tone (HRV), a wristband, bracelet, or simply measure the time it takes to lower the heart rate after exercise can help. By taking regular action, we will be able to monitor our progress.

In addition, several activities are known to increase vagal tone:

- Sing

- Consumption of fermented foods
- Physical exercise, especially that which is intense
- The sauna or having a hot bath, followed by a cold shower
- Laughter
- Cold showers and ice baths
- Hugs, connecting with other people
- Breathing exercises, one of them can be a physiological sigh
- Practice yoga
- Let you meditate

The vagus nerve helps you calm down, exercise calms, and even something as simple as taking time for yourself each day will improve the vagus nerve. This will help you cope better with challenging moments.

The lower part of our brain is made up of a complex network of nerves called cranial nerves. There are 12 in total, each with a name depending on their origin, activity, or the specific function they fulfill. The vagus nerve enters number 10 and is responsible for sending information related to muscle sensitivity and activity.

This nerve is the longest of all cranial nerves. It descends from a low level in the head to the abdomen and is called the pneumoperitoneal nerve. Along its route, it produces several branches that intervene in various organs.

The vagus nerve, among other things, interacts with the immune system and the central nervous system and performs motor functions in the larynx, diaphragm, stomach, and heart. It also has the sensory function of internal organs such as the ears, tongue, and liver.

When the vagus nerve is functioning properly, it helps us manage stress and anxiety and promotes calm. When its function is altered by disease, tumor, trauma, neurodegenerative disease, autoimmune disease, diabetes, etc., vagal tone decreases, and dysphagia, migraine, hoarseness, digestive disorders, high blood pressure, epilepsy, etc. may occur. Also, there are other psychological or psychiatric types, such as anxiety, depression, stress, and addictive tendencies, to name a few.

When the vagus nerve is altered, it produces exaggerated emotional responses and fails to activate relaxation signals. The sympathetic nervous system (responsible for controlling certain organs in situations that require rapid activation of their functions, reflexes, and visceral responses) does not relax and remains active, so the person reacts impulsively and suffers anxiety and stress.

CHAPTER #4: 30 WAYS OF EXERCISE TO NAVIGATE AND STRETCH YOUR VAGUS NERVE

This is a series of exercises you can do to stimulate and stretch the vagus nerve, backed by science.

Nature Therapy

Naturopathy, or "forest bathing," as the Japanese called it, can help your body relax. How? You just go into nature and walk. Forest baths are based on conscious and quiet walks in the forest, where you allow yourself to experience the environment with all your senses. You can walk for 15 minutes through the forest to reduce cortisol levels and blood pressure.

Breathing

Breathing is a tool that has a lot of power, just breathing deeply can help you stretch and activate the vagus nerve. This can help to calm you down and stimulate your nervous system. There are a variety of breathing techniques that help you with for health. Here are some of them:

- You concentrate on deep breaths, carefully follow the air you inhale, and exhale through your nose, lungs, and abdomen.
- Proceed to take six deep breaths from the diaphragm in the span of one minute. The exhalations should be long and slow so that you stretch them little by little.
- Inhale slowly through your nose while counting to 5, exhale slowly through your nose, and count to 5. You will wait 5 seconds and repeat the process 3 more times.

This has great benefit, according to a study called self-regulation of breathing through the vagus nerve of Communication research conducted by Dr. Joseph Breuer at the Institute of Physiology of the Royal Academy of Emperor Joseph.

Take a Hot Bath

According to studies, it is known that immersion in water at 102°F/38°C helps reduce the response of the sympathetic nervous system, which calms the body from heat. If you put Epsom salts, you will increase magnesium levels, which helps you lead to relaxing. To make your bath even more relaxing, you can put in some essential bath oils and put on relaxing music that you like. In this way, you will involve your senses more in this relaxation process.

Play Relaxing Music

Music will help you activate the parasympathetic nervous system because it calms the brain. Listening to relaxing music helps you with blood pressure, heart rate, and breathing rate. Certain musical frequencies have been confirmed to have more benefits than others. Some studies show that listening to music at 432 Hz relaxes much more than listening to music at 440 Hz, the frequency at which most modern music is tuned.

A study called *Music Intervention for Psychological Trauma: A Proposal Psychologist*, made by an expert in Clinical and Intervention in Trauma with EMDR by the Spanish Society of Psychosomatic Medicine and Psychotherapy Ana de la Mata San Marcos, confirms that music gives many benefits to stretch and stimulate the vagus nerve.

Hug a Human/Pet

Hugging a loved one activates the parasympathetic nervous system, which releases serotonin, dopamine, and oxytocin. In particular, oxytocin is the chemical of love and union. When you have a loved one around, you just have to go and give them a warm hug from time to time, and you will see how they make you feel. If you have pets? They like to give hugs too! Pets are really therapeutic and serve to reduce stress or increase happy hormones.

Do Absolutely Nothing

Doing nothing helps you with the nervous system because it helps you process your thoughts and feelings and then release them. If you find it difficult to do anything, you can start with 2 minutes. Don't look at your phone, eat, or get distracted! Because you can get frustrated at first, with the brain trying to get sidetracked by whatever happens near you (the phone, the TV, or whatever you think about), but that's normal; that's how our busy brains work.

Look to see what is crossing your head and do nothing. You'll notice that it's harder than you think, but remember: that's where your nervous system is finally free of any external stimuli and can calm down.

Aromatherapy

Aromatherapy research demonstrates the ability for you to create homeostasis in the nervous system and calm anxiety. Bergamot and lavender have been shown to help you a lot in reducing stress. You can smell them, spread them and even find perfumes that smell like them! If you have essential oils such as lavender, patchouli, valerian, bergamot, marjoram, or rose, simply put them in your bath and enjoy their relaxing effects. Some of these can also be added to massage oils.

It has been proven to have benefits according to the study called Aromatherapy in the mental health of Marilú Roxana Soto-Vásquez; Paul Alan Arkin Alvarado-Garcia; William Antonio Sagastegui-Guarniz describing the evidence for and against the use of aromatherapy in stress, anxiety, depression, sleep disorders, cognitive impairment, and other disorders. In addition to data related to what helps and mechanisms of action, aromatherapy can be taken as an option that can be used as an adjunct to treatments aimed at restoring mental health and related disorders.

Listening to the Birds

Birds sing when there are no predators nearby. Their singing helps calm the nervous system because it tells us that there is no danger nearby. Birdsong is part of having that contact with nature, which calms your nervous system. Imagine you stand on the green grass on a warm, sunny day, and all you can hear is birds chirping. Sounds relaxing?

Gardening

Any hobby can give you peace or joy and has the power to bring you to a calm state. You can do gardening because it allows you to be in contact with nature and sunlight at the same time, which is proven to calm us. Beyond that, it offers you the opportunity to limit the stressors around you (it's hard to grow flowers in the garden and discuss with your boss over the phone) and focus on this relaxing activity.

Sun Exposure

Sunny colors help you soothe. They also serve to regulate circadian rhythms through melatonin production and lower cortisol levels. When you expose yourself to the sun, the number of neurotransmitters, such as serotonin increases, which leaves you with a positive effect on health.

Sauna

Taking 15-minute sauna sessions has been shown to help lower cortisol levels and induce the parasympathetic nervous system. The heat you encounter in the sauna helps you with many different health problems. If you haven't, you can start with 5 minutes and gradually increase the time. Don't forget to drink plenty of water (drink plenty of water during the sauna) to make you healthier and help.

Down to Earth

Having contact with the earth allows you to absorb negative ions from the earth, which are like antioxidants. Research shows that when your feet touch the ground, your muscles start to relax, leading to the parasympathetic nervous system being activated to work. The earth releases negative ions in your body, which have a positive effect, such as improving sleep, calming inflammation, helping with blood flow, and even improving tissue and cell repair.

It is enough that you go out to an area of land like the mountain and walk or that the gardening is done in contact with the earth.

Sewing

Sewing has the power to put us in a state of flow. It forces a person to focus on the task at hand and allows hand-eye coordination to attract attention. Sewing is a great escape from the stress of everyday life! It also keeps you away from everyday distractions, such as the phone, TV, or work, which are often common sources of stress. It will also give you extra satisfaction if you end up sewing a new t-shirt.

Meditation

There is evidence that meditation helps calm stress and anxiety and stretches the vagus nerve. It can help reduce our ability to respond to stress that is out of our control. Many studies have shown the positive effects of various meditation techniques or methods, such as calming mindfulness-based stress (MBSR). Meditation serves to control triggers and breathing, reduces blood pressure and stress on the heart, lactic acid in the muscles, and can even cope with pain. It improves sleep, reduces stress, and helps relieve strong and difficult emotions. You can try different meditation methods and choose the one that works best for you.

This has been shown in many studies, for example, one called Goodbye to the Polyvagal Theory of the Psyscience site. To do this, start like this:

- You sit on the floor comfortably with your legs bent. You put one foot on your thigh in the lotus position or in a chair, whatever you want.
- Being in this position, concentrate on the breath, inhaling and exhaling, observing the entire path of the air. Now pay attention to the sensations that are coming.
- Try to concentrate on what the body says and what the vagus nerve does, imagine that it stretches little by little and relaxes, that it calms you down, and gives you well-being.

This is an exercise you can use to scan your entire body and heal it.

Yawning

Scientists have proven that yawning is a signal for you to activate the parasympathetic nervous system, which reduces stress and calms the risk of high blood pressure. If you yawn, you can consciously bring your body into this state of rest and digestion. However, you can think about yawning and doing it several times, such as when you try to uncover your plugged ears when you are traveling.

Yawning is one of the exercise options found in the study *Techniques for the Control of Activation, relaxation, and Breathing*, by Mariano Chóliz Montañés

Draw/Doodle

Creating art is an easy way to induce a parasympathetic state because you focus on what you're creating. Draw, doodle, or sculpt the parasympathetic nervous system for the power to bring calm and happiness. It can restore you and help with energy levels. Painting, or any other type of art, is a way to express yourself and express all the emotions you carry. Are you angry, stressed, sad, or excited? Take a pen and release emotions on paper. It doesn't have to be pretty, just start drawing!

Reading

Reading has the power to put you in a parasympathetic state by participating. It allows you to focus on one thing and leave stress behind. If you do it before bed, it can help you relax and prepare for sleep. There are a variety of books that can be read that can help you feel more relaxed in different ways. A good comedy will make you laugh; an addictive novel will take you to another world; an informational book is going to teach you something new about an interesting topic: these are just some of the ways reading can help you.

Pray

It has been shown in studies that parasympathetic nerves are activated while sympathetic nerves decrease during prayer. This puts the person into resting and digesting mode, reducing anxiety and cardiovascular risk. We usually pray in a quiet place or surrounded by other prayers. In both cases, we have the opportunity to focus solely on this activity without being distracted by anything else. This can take us out of fight-or-flight mode and calm our minds.

Qigong

Qigong is a method of physical exercise that has its roots in ancient China and has been approved by the Chinese government as a healing technique. Activate the flow state by making use of breathing, correct posture, and good focus. There are many types of Qigong, but all serve to put you in a state of natural harmony and take care of your health.

The easiest way to do this is to inhale, counting to four, and exhale, counting to six. You will enter the phase in about five minutes and you will be able to help your vagus nerve.

Visualization

Relaxed images have the power to help the parasympathetic state get going, it collaborates with the body to feel that something happens in reality. You can use your memories, and you will move with your imagination to places where you once felt relaxed and at peace. If you imagine yourself on a sunny beach, your brain is going to trick you into feeling like you're there!

Find a quiet and comfortable place, close your eyes, and discover the power of your imagination. Take some time. You'll be surprised how relaxing it feels. You can visualize the vagus nerve, the calmness of your fears, what overwhelms you, see how it resolves, see as if it has already happened, and you will see how you will feel better soon.

Mantras

When you notice your mind wandering, you can use a mantra to bring your mind back to reality. This helps you create a sense of security and calm the body. You can repeat "I'm safe" several times to get a positive effect. A Mantra has been shown to have a calming effect on the nervous system. One of the most well-known mantras is OM, which has a frequency of 432 hertz and slows down the nervous system, calms the mind, and promotes mindfulness.

You can put yourself in meditation mode and repeat the mantra, feeling that a sound is coming from the chest OMMMMMM; with practice, you will feel that your chest vibrates when you say it.

Healing Music: Proven Through Medical Research Memorial Cancer Center Sloan Kettering is a study where among other methods, mantras have been tested.

Stretch

Stretching increases blood flow and dilates blood vessels in the muscles. It is known that the mind can be influenced by our body, and stretching is proof of all this. Stress is often built up in our bodies. Thanks to stretching, you will release all tension. This mechanism helps the body relax in a parasympathetic state.

It is enough that you slowly stand up and raise your arms, stretching them forcefully toward the sky as if you wanted to touch them. Stretch your feet slowly, your fingers, your neck, and every part of your body.

Touch Your Lips Gently

Your lips have parasympathetic nerve fibers that run through them, and they can be stimulated by running your finger through your lips! In addition, it turns out that our mouth can improve our mood. How? Look for a pen and have it horizontally in your mouth so that it immediately looks like your smile. Research shows that your brain recognizes it as a smile and adjusts emotions accordingly. Try this so you feel the effects immediately.

Yoga

Yoga activates the parasympathetic nervous system because it improves the fight-or-flight response. People who do yoga often feel their emotions relieved. This is due to faster recognition of the body's stress. Like any other physical activity, yoga helps you a lot in the body and mind. However, yoga is more than just doing asanas. Pranayamas are breathing techniques with advantages that help you activate the parasympathetic nervous system and make you feel calm. If you are new to yoga and pranayama, it is best to start practicing under the guidance of an experienced teacher.

To try it, you will sit in a comfortable upright position with your eyes closed gently, preferably on a mat or where you sit comfortably, with your legs crossed. Take a breath, then exhale with a "buzzing" sound. This will generate vibrations in the center of your body, which stimulates the vagus nerve.

It will also generate a similar effect to the "woo" sound. I advise you to try to focus the vibrations just behind the navel, then stop for a moment to notice what sensations, thoughts, feelings, or images are manifested. Feel free to repeat this three times.

According to a study by the University of La Laguna, called *Stress and Psychological Health,* yoga as a complementary therapy, and the benefits of doing yoga for the vagus nerve are shown.

Get Enough Sleep

Getting enough rest is good for several health reasons, as it serves to rest and recover. During sleep, blood circulation rises, as does oxygen and nutrients. With the mind and sense of calm, you will rest. Getting enough sleep is good for our nervous system to work properly. Remember how you feel after you rest. I don't think I need to convince you of the importance of getting enough sleep.

Cold Water Immersion

Exposure to cold water or compresses can help stimulate the vagus nerve because the shock of cold water activates the sympathetic nervous system.

A small 2018 study found that cold stimulation can help reduce stress by slowing the heart rate and directing blood flow to the brain. The effect of cold stimulation is most pronounced in the neck area.

With this in mind, Dr. Thomas Adams, a board-certified psychiatrist and psychotherapist at Menlo Park Psychiatry & Sleep Medicine recommends:

- Place cold on the front or sides of the neck, or in the center of the upper chest.
- Place your face in cold water.
- Take a cold shower or switch to cold water for the last 2 to 5 minutes of your shower.

Exercise

Exercise, which you can do in activities that raise your heart rate, is a great way to strengthen your vagus nerve. A small 2016 study found that those who participated in riding a bicycle had increased vagal nerve activity.

You can also do the following:

- Brisk walking
- Weightlifting
- Swim
- Pilates

According to the study, cardiovascular training is one of the best ways to get the vagus nerve to work because it requires you to work hard to control your breathing. It puts your body in a hyperactive state and then activates the vagus nerve so that you return it to a calm state.

However, be careful not to overtrain. A small 2022 study found that excessively intense workouts, such as too much high-intensity interval training (HIIT), put a lot of pressure on the vagus nerve.

Take these tips into account:

- Listen to your body and the limits you begin to overcome.
- Confirm placing breathing exercises and cool-downs when training.
- Take breaks.

Vagus Nerve Stimulation Device

Vagus nerve stimulation devices help with the vagus nerve that gives electrical impulses and grows specific neurotransmitters in the brain. This causes vagus nerve function to rise. It is advantageous for people with severe epilepsy, depression, or conditions. There are several devices available, and as research on them grows, there will be more.

Laughter Therapy

Laughter therapy has a great positive stimulating power on the vagus nerve. Joy and positive emotions that relate to social activities can improve vagal tone. Laughter is also a great medicine for stressful situations. Sometimes releasing stress with a funny joke helps you calm that emotion or misbehave.

Laughter, an essential complement in the patient's recovery is a work by Jennifer Jaimes, Andrea Claro, Sergio Perea, and Erika Jaimes, published in revistas.uis where she talks about how laughter helps the vagus nerve.

Play Outdoors with Others

Natural remedies are shown to be very good at reducing stress responses and leading to a parasympathetic state. Playing with others creates a sense of camaraderie that serves to calm your nervous system. You get plenty of fresh air and higher levels of endorphins thanks to the outdoors.

Doing it is simple, you can spend some time playing with your children, nephews, cousins, or whoever you want; you can even do it on your own.

Watch Sunset/Sunrise

Watching a sunset or sunrise helps regulate circadian rhythms. Having some sun first thing in the morning can reduce your cortisol response and allow you to sleep better at night. It also helps you appreciate the little things in life for simple pleasures. You can combine this with small rituals like morning exercise, meditation, or a good cup of tea to give yourself some time to consciously experience these simple pleasures.

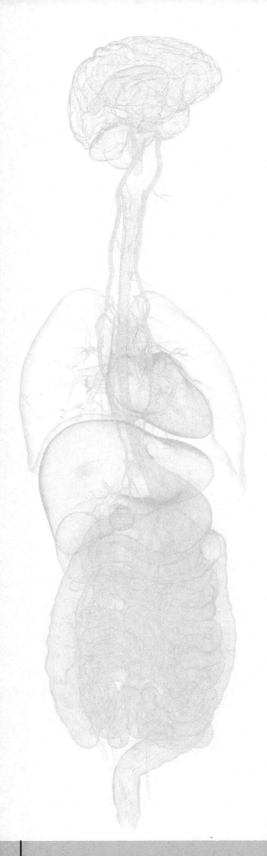

CHAPTER #5: 5-MINUTE VAGUS NERVE EXERCISES FOR BUSY PEOPLE

If you have little time in the day to do longer exercises, such as taking a yoga class, I share some exercises that you can do from your workplace or in a few free minutes.

Physical Exercises of the Vagus Nerve

These exercises that you will see below are focused on working the vocal cords. The physical reverberation of the cords helps the vagus nerve.

Gargle

You rinse your mouth with water when you brush your teeth in the morning and evening. You're going to do a test from 30 seconds to 1 minute. Just as you would with rinsing or when you make a remedy, you consciously apply it.

Sing a Song

No matter if it's a piece of song, a chorus, or several songs (or make the dog howl to the rhythm of your melody), start singing what you want in some space at home or in the office!

Om -ing

Yes, you apply with the Om that relates to the practice of yoga. You sit in a quiet place and do a long "Om." You have to feel a vibration around your ear, which is connected to the vagus nerve. A study in the International Journal of Yoga found that chanting "om" helps shut down parts of the brain's limbic system, such as the amygdala, involved in stress and emotional responses.

Try to Laugh During the Day

You can watch a funny TV show or movie and laugh at the funny parts. Or, hang out with your always happy friends to have a little laugh.

Psychological Exercises of the Vagus Nerve

However, for the vagus nerve to be in action is not the only way to activate it: your thoughts and feelings can trigger it. It generates an emotional response that supports the vagus nerve and calms the parasympathetic nervous system.

Gratitude Journal

You sit down before you go to bed or when you wake up and write down three things you are grateful for, whether they are big (your family) or small (the delicious latte you drink early). Repeat this rhythm daily, weekly, or at any other suitable for you to start the vagus nerve.

Deep Breathing

This is a breathing exercise you can do. It is known as square breathing. Take a breath and count to 4, you will hold while counting to 4, release the air while counting to 4, and hold while counting to 4. You repeat as many times as you consider. Take a deep breath to make the body think, "If I breathe so slowly, I can't escape."

A Little Meditation

Meditation can be done in many ways and doesn't have to be long, or the prologue to a yoga session, but studies have shown that meditation and "contemplative practices" like yoga calm you down, in part by activating the vagus nerve. Take five minutes for a short-guided meditation on apps or a YouTube one that tells you step by step. Put on your headphones and enjoy it.

See Beautiful Things Like a Sunset

Exposure to beautiful things like a sunset, spending time in nature, seeing beautiful images, or playing with pets, anything that triggers positive emotions, varies from person to person, increases vagal tone, and has been found to help improve physical health, notes a randomized controlled trial in Psychological Science.

Long Exhalations to Let Go of Mind and Body

Just inhaling a longer exhalation stimulates the vagus nerve. By the way, a study in the International Journal of Psychophysiology showed that taking a slow, deep two-minute breath increases vagus nerve activity, allowing for more time between heartbeats. In turn, this can result in better decision-making!

Prolonged exhalation sends a message to the brain through the vagus nerve that your body can calm down and, according to mindfulness, leads to the stillness of mind and body and can even induce sleep.

As you lie down, take a breath and exhale, take a breath counting to four, then let go counting to four. Gradually inhale four times and release five times, gradually inhale four times and exhale eight times on a ratio of 1:2. It's so effective that you'll fall asleep before you know it!

Neck Lifts to Tone the Vagus Nerve

If you send security messages to the brain, it will trigger positive emotions. Since many of us live in constant tension, I advise you this simple neck massage.

This will also stretch the sternocleidomastoid muscle, a thick muscle that runs along the side of the neck. People with migraines often feel tension in this area.

Put your right hand over your head and gently tilt your head and right ear toward your right shoulder. Now raise your head and leave it in position for 30 seconds, and then you will repeat on the other side.

Stretching the Torso Activates the Vagus Nerve

This yoga exercise starts the vagus nerve in the torso and moves the thoracic region, and makes the nervous system stable. You sit on the floor or in a chair and turn around. Put your right hand on the outside of your left leg and behind you your left hand. Go over your left shoulder. You will straighten the spine when you inhale and deepen the turn when you release the air. Then it switches sides.

Ear Massage to Soothe

The ear is connected by the upper side of the vagus nerve. While this may seem like a small movement, this area can affect tension. Since the vagus nerve also connects to the throat and chest, when toned, the neck can relax, and sinus breathing becomes easier.

You will put your fingers gently on the crest of the ear canal and move it with gentle circular movements. You repeat it on the other side. Then, gently remove the ear from the skull, moving it up and down. This will help relieve temporomandibular joint pain and any discomfort you may have.

Now massage the area behind the ear, move your fingers up and down, and repeat on the other side. When you massage this area, you send relaxation messages to the brain through the vagus nerve.

Breathing Practice

Slow breathing and extensive exhalations stimulate the vagus nerve, which is why this technique works so well. Even small amounts of stress can trigger physiological responses in the body, including increased heart rate, shallow breathing, and muscle tension. When you extend the exhalation, you will calm the nerves, have control of the heart rate, and improve your skills to make decisions. You can do it whenever you want to relax or calm down.

1. For the next few minutes, allow yourself to focus only on yourself. Find a comfortable place in a quiet and safe space and sit down. You can do this exercise sitting or lying down. You can close your eyes if you want. Refocus your attention on your breath and at this moment.
2. On your next breath, inhale through your nose and exhale through pursed lips. Keep inhaling through your nose and exhaling through your mouth for the rest of the exercise.
3. The next time you inhale, extend your inhalation to four, then exhale to four. Do this for 3 rounds.
4. The duration of exhalation now doubles. Inhale to the count of 4. Exhale to the account of 8. Do this for the rest of the exercises.
5. When you're ready to finish the exercise, move your fingers and toes to get your breathing back to its normal rhythm.
6. Pay attention to how you feel physically and mentally. Check out these steps again the next time you want to practice 4:8 breathing.

Humming Practice

For you to activate the vagus nerve with this exercise, you will slow down your breathing and produce a low buzzing sound when you exhale. The buzzing vibrations send a signal to the vagus nerve and generate a relaxation response. You may feel locked up or overwhelmed, but this exercise will help you calm your nervous system and put in a balance to tone.

1. No matter where you are right now, take a moment to notice where your body is. Take the time to find a sitting or standing position that is aligned and comfortable. We're going to do two rounds of humming. We inhale, then we start exhaling, then we inhale again, and we do it again.
2. Inhale fully and exhale with a low hum. Pause and let the next inhalation flow naturally. Inhale completely with a low hum while releasing the air. Repeat this as many times as possible.
3. Take a break now and see how your body feels. Take a moment to notice your breathing, any changes in muscle tone, and how thoughts slow down for a moment.

Fire Breathing

This exercise is ideal for the vagus nerve because it serves to release tension in the neck and shoulders. It also makes circulation better, increases the amount of energy, and helps reduce stress and anxiety.

To do this, you must:

☒ Sit on the floor or in a chair.

☒ Put your back straight while putting your hands on your stomach.

☒ Take a deep breath through your nose so that your body stretches like a balloon.

☒ Blow little by little through the mouth while you are squeezing your stomach.

☒ Repeat this 3 to 5 times for 30 seconds.

Penguin Walk

Walking will help the vagus nerve because it sends signals from the brain to the muscles that help you move your arms and legs.

Among the benefits are:

- ☒ Improves balance.

- ☒ Improves coordination.

- ☒ Reduce stress.

- ☒ Reduces anxiety.

To do so:

1. You're going to stand on one leg with your arms at your sides.

2. Raise the other leg off the floor and do a knee flexion so that the thigh is parallel to the ground.

3. Then you will walk forward little by little, keeping your raised leg bent at the knee. Make sure to keep your arms at your sides and focus on maintaining balance.

4. When you reach the end of the room, you turn around and walk back to the starting position.

5. Do this exercise again several times, changing legs each time.

Breathing Pause

The main reason breathing this way is so good for the vagus nerve is that it makes you breathe deeper and slower. This has many advantages, as it helps you reduce your heart rate and blood pressure, which are the key risk factors for many types of health problems.

Some benefits of breathing pause:

- ☒ Calms the nervous system.

- ☒ Promotes relaxation.

- ☒ Increases blood flow to the brain.

To do this you must:

1. You're just going to sit or lie down in a comfortable position.

2. Take a deep breath and leave it for a few seconds.
3. Release the air little by little and repeat the process.
4. You may find this breathing challenging at first. But with practice, you'll be able to hold your breath for longer periods of time.

Carotid Sinus Massage

This exercise is about massaging the carotid sinuses, which are pressure points on the sides of the neck. Carotid sinus function helps regulate blood pressure and heart rate. You can do it several times a day.

Here's how:

1. You sit or stand in a comfortable position.

2. Gently massage the carotid sinus with your fingers for 30 seconds.

3. You repeat it on the other side of the neck.

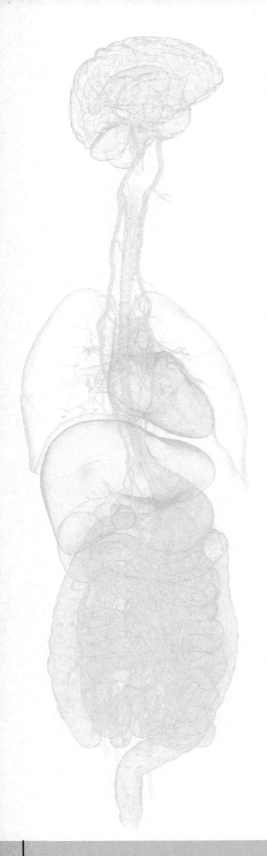

CHAPTER #6: VAGUS NERVE EXERCISES FOR HEALTH PROBLEMS

These exercises will help calm any condition you have that comes from a vagus nerve that is not well-stimulated and balanced.

Sternocleidomastoid Stretching

This stretch feels good and involves stretching the sternocleidomastoid muscle in your neck. If sagging shoulders can be caused by ankylosing spondylitis, doing this exercise frequently can help strengthen the trapezius muscles.

Benefits of stretching sternocleidomastoid:

- Reduce neck pain.
- Relieve tension headaches.

Here's how to do it:

1. You sit in a comfortable position.
2. Put your left hand on your left shoulder.
3. Use your right hand to gently pull your head toward your right shoulder. You will feel a stretch on the left side of your neck.
4. You will leave this stretch for 30 seconds.
5. You're going to repeat on the other side.

Pelvic Tilt

Pelvic tilts help release tension in the lower back and relieve sciatica pain. You'll also stretch your hip flexors, which can become strained from sitting for too long.

Here's how:

1. You start lying on your back.

2. You leave your feet flat on the floor.

3. You put your back flat on the floor and tighten your abdominal muscles.

4. Leave this posture for three to five seconds.

5. Make a release and relax the abdominal muscles.

6. Do repetitions at least five times.

Foot in a Supine Position

This exercise helps vagal tone by using your breath to put your body in a relaxed state.

This is how you do it:

1. You will lie on your back in a position where you feel comfortable.

2. Put your feet flat on the floor.

3. Stretch your arms above your head with your fingers intertwined.

4. Slowly raise your head and shoulders from the ground.

5. Use your abdominal muscles to get your legs up from the floor. Leave your knees straight.

6. Place this pose for five seconds.

7. It relaxes and releases the muscles of the abdomen.

8. Repeat five times.

Cat Pose

The cat's posture will stimulate the vagus nerve by raising blood flow to the head and neck.

Here are the steps:

1. You start by putting your hands and knees in the table position.

2. Make sure your wrists are placed directly under your shoulders and your knees are directly under your hips.

3. Turn your back towards the ceiling, and bring your chin closer to your chest.

4. Hold this posture for five seconds.

5. Relaxes and releases the muscles of the back.

6. Repeat five times.

Child Posture

Extend your knees and sit on your heels. Stretch your arms in front of you, allowing your chest to reintegrate into the mat. Take several deep breaths for you to calm your body; you relax more deeply with each exhalation. Leave the Child Posture counting to ten, breathing deeply in this way.

Forward Fold

Stand on your mat. With your feet hip-width apart, roll your upper body over your thighs. Let your arms hang heavily, allowing you to bend your knees slightly and rest your stomach on your thighs in a relaxed posture. Let your neck relax, and let the crown of your head fall back on the mat. Hold here for ten breaths.

Compatible Heart Opener

If you don't have a rolled-up mat or blanket, put it vertically in the center of the mat. Put the short side of the brace over your tailbone and lie on your back, allowing the brace to make room for your heart. You can do this with your legs spread or your feet together in a reclining butterfly pose. Take ten deep breaths here.

Waterfall

You remove the reinforcement, lie on a mat and put a yoga block under the coccyx. Extend your legs towards the ceiling, keeping your knees slightly bent, and get in a cascading position. Leave your legs soft and relaxed while letting the rest of your body sink into the ground. You can stretch your ankle further by turning your foot in one direction and then in the other. Hold ten breaths.

Happy Baby

Remove the block and lie on the mat. Extend your legs to the ceiling and hold the outer edges of your feet, bringing your knees closer to your armpits. Root yourself firmly in your spine and take breaths. Hold here or invite gentle movement to the pose, rock back and forth along the spine, or extend one leg and then the other for you to stretch your hamstrings. Hold ten breaths.

Savasana

You lie on your back and leave your arms and legs apart. Take a few deep breaths through your nose and mouth. Proceed to release any breath control or seek to control your mind and let your body release the tensions you are holding. You stay here for you to absorb the effects of your practice for up to ten minutes, then you leave gently and get back to your day when you're done.

Conscious Breathing

The most direct way to alter the balance of activity in the sympathetic and parasympathetic nervous systems is breathing. To counteract any overstimulation of the sympathetic nervous system, vagal yoga is focused on diaphragmatic breathing and prolongs the duration of the exhalation. Research has found that slow, rhythmic diaphragmatic breathing promotes healthy vagal tone. One form of yogic breathing is Ujjayi pranayama, which generates a small contraction in the back of the throat by activating the whispering muscles. To learn this breath, exhale through your mouth as if you were fogging a mirror. Now, breathe the same way, but close your mouth and exhale through your nose. You will notice that your breathing becomes louder, often sounding like the waves of the sea. Start by counting inhalations and exhalations evenly. To make you relax more deeply, gradually increase the duration of the exhalation compared to its inhalation. For example, you could start by counting to 4 when inhaling and count to 6 or 8 when exhaling. This will calm your parasympathetic nervous system down.

Half Smile

Practicing a "half smile" is an invaluable way to change the way you think and develop a sense of serenity in the present moment. Since the vagus nerve enters the facial muscles, it is possible to increase vagal tone by relaxing the facial muscles and then gently raising the lips. This practice helps you activate what's known as the "social nervous system," the most evolved branch of the vagus nerve. When you smile, imagine that your jaw softens and relaxation spreads across your face, head, and shoulders. Notice subtle changes in the quality of thoughts and emotions.

Wake Up and Stretch

If you have trouble getting out of bed in the morning or feel tired and lethargic in the afternoon, yoga will gently lift your body and mind. Explore standing postures like the warrior pose (virabhadrasana) to invigorate your mind and awaken your body. Be careful to ground both feet and stay grounded and energized in a balanced way. Keep your breathing rhythmic so you can stay grounded and in touch with how your body feels.

Release the Belly

You can work on the vagus nerve as it travels through your abdomen. Find the position of the table with your hands under your shoulders and your knees below your hips. If you experience any discomfort in your knees, put a folded blanket under you. As you inhale, begin to raise your head and hips, pressing your belly toward the ground as you enter the cow's pose. As you exhale, lift your spine to the cat's pose while lowering your head and hips. Use your breath to find your rhythm of movement. Repeat several times, gently massaging the abdomen and spine.

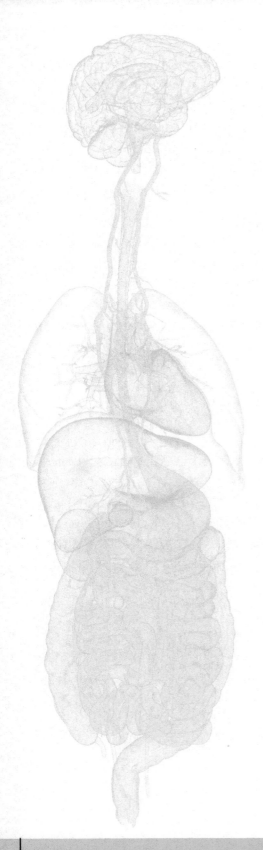

CHAPTER #7: VAGUS NERVE STIMULATION FOR DEPRESSION

If you have depression, some of the origins may be from the vagus nerve, which among its symptoms includes mental health problems. Let's look at these exercises you can do.

Control Breathing

Breathing is one of the most effective ways to put yourself in charge of your experience. When you change the dynamics of your breathing, you enter a feedback loop that would otherwise exacerbate stress. During the inspiratory phase of breathing, the heart rate increases. When you exhale, the vagus nerve slows the heartbeat interval through its influence on the parasympathetic nervous system. The slower you exhale, the calmer you will feel.

Since breathing influences stress levels, the researchers explored how breathing affects the vagus nerve and even decision-making. In their study, published in the International Journal of Psychophysiology, comparisons were made of how different types of breathing affected subjects' responses to a stress test that added up, leading to mild depression. One group performed a "tilted" breathing pattern (exhaling for a longer time compared to inhaling), while the other group did not.

Although the task significantly increased physical stress markers in the second group, those who did the flexed breathing pattern answered the test questions quickly, more accurately, and showed fewer signs of physiological stress.

The study showed that even brief changes in breathing dynamics could help with depression in the body, changing the way we respond to those day-to-day challenges.

Rapid Breathing Changes: 4-7-8 Technique

Dr. Andrew Weil, a functional medicine practitioner, designed the 4-7-8 breathing technique, which consists of the method of breath control using the ancient tradition of pranayama. This technique is one of the easiest and fastest types of breathing as it helps you quickly reduce exhalation.

Researchers were able to demonstrate its healing properties in many conditions, including pain during childbirth or after surgery. It also helps release feelings of depression and supports focus during or before creative expression.

How to do it:

1. You're going to sit comfortably with your back supported. You put your tongue in the place where the gum is with the upper front teeth and leave it there for the whole exercise.

2. The first step is to exhale completely with a whistling sound.

3. You do it for 4 seconds, inhale calmly through the nose, and focus on breathing from the diaphragm instead of from the chest.

4. Then hold your breath for seven seconds.

5. Release the air forcefully through the lips set in rounded and hold for eight seconds.

6. This would be a round.

The goal of the exercise is to extend the exhalation twice as long as the inhalation process. A starting point that I advise is four rounds for you to feel the changes, putting in more as you gain experience with the practice.

Sing, Humming

The vagus nerve has the job of controlling the muscles of the larynx (vocal cords) that help sound be produced. Mechanically, the act of singing demands that you exhale more than you inhale. So, when you do, you hum or psalmody, you generate vibrations that automatically create a stimulus in the throat muscles that connect to the vagus nerve. These influences give it meaning given the history shared with music. Paleolithic evidence suggests that our species has been making music for at least 40,000 years.

In addition to singing or humming, just listening to music can also stimulate the vagus nerve. Music psychologists have shown many times that certain structural or tonal aspects of music can lead to reliable emotional and physiological responses in listeners.

For example, a recent study called *Music as Medicine* looked at how 7581 participants made use of music for self-regulation. They tested whether specific qualities of music (such as tempo, genre, lyric content, etc.) could reliably calm feelings of depression and, if so, how long a person needed to listen to enjoy these effects.

They discovered something they called a therapeutic dose of music: a set of qualities a song needs to reliably induce attention, relaxation, or pleasure. When it came to calming down, they found that the best music was slow, without lyrics, and with simple melodies. They found that the ideal listening time was 13 minutes.

At the moment those who participated listened to music with these qualities:

- ☒ 79.20% said they felt less muscle tension.

- ☒ 84.31% already thought less negatively, and their depression was calmer.

- ☒ 91.69% felt a greater sense of satisfaction.

- ☒ 82.30% slept better.

All of this suggests that the benefits of music extend far beyond entertainment or self-expression: creating or listening to music also helps you alter your body naturally, process your emotions, and take control of what you're feeling.

One way to stimulate the vagus nerve with music is to consult the therapeutic playlists used in previous studies. The researchers documented the playlist's success in relaxing, concentrating, coping with grief, and increasing feelings of well-being. Music "with the added vitamins of sound" (as they say) can also help you focus or create a relaxing atmosphere before bed. Music can even affect athletic performance due to its calming effects on the nervous system. Studies have shown that listening to music during a workout can better activate the parasympathetic nervous system during recovery, meaning it can help you move into rest and digestion mode more quickly after an intense workout.

Recovering faster helps you enjoy vagus nerve benefits, such as greater mental clarity and endurance while reducing the negative effects of stress on the body.

Loving-Kindness Meditation Practice

When you have trouble focusing because you have depressive thoughts, does it have to do with fear of judgment or criticism? Almost all of us have, at some point, been overwhelmed by "social judgment stress," which is the strain caused by performance anxiety or criticism from friends or family.

Thanks to this kind of feeling that is so common in life, social psychologists have long had ways to lessen the negative effects of depression on the body. Previous research has proven that the trait of self-compassion, or the power to show kindness and understanding toward oneself, has stress-relieving properties even in the face of social evaluation.

Based on this information, in a study published in the *Journal of Psychoneuroendocrinology*, researchers tested whether a five-minute Buddhist meditation of self-compassion for 40 days changed the responses of those who participated in a depression test. These self-compassion exercises are based on a practice called "Metta," which means loving kindness in Pali, an ancient Buddhist meditation designed to evoke a state of love for oneself and others.

To practice metta, breathe slowly, feel comfortable, and eliminate distractions as you normally would. Instead of just focusing on how your body is feeling or calming your mind, remember your loved ones with joy. It can be a father, a daughter, an old friend, a dog, etc.

Try to focus on an easy relationship so that tension doesn't distract you. Say phrases like this when you think of the person:

- Maybe you're happy.

- May you be healthy.

- Let you know that joys and struggles are shared by others.

After you focus on your loved one, it is often recommended that they direct feelings toward you by sending love and understanding from your own experiences. You can gradually broaden your attention, turning to people you find neutral, such as strangers or colleagues, and gradually bring all sentient beings into your thoughts.

Research into the biological effects of Metta has increased greatly over the past decade, with studies showing the advantages in relieving depression and anxiety, to name just two of the many benefits.

Touch to Relieve Feelings of Depression

Also, the vagus nerve can be stimulated through touch. Our fifth sense, touch, has great power in this part of the body. Depending on factors such as speed, pressure, and vibration, touch generates body and biochemical changes that help improve well-being, concentration, and resistance to pain, among other profound effects.

Touch works on the vagus nerve thanks to the interconnections that occur in the vagal fibers and pressure detectors in the skin. The vagal fibers connect with the vagal systems of the brain and are involved in the regulation of the nervous system and the secretion of stress hormones such as cortisol.

Massaging someone else helps with the same baroreceptors on your fingers that kick in when you get a touch. For the same reason, giving or receiving a hug or massage or petting a beloved dog or cat can be relaxing.

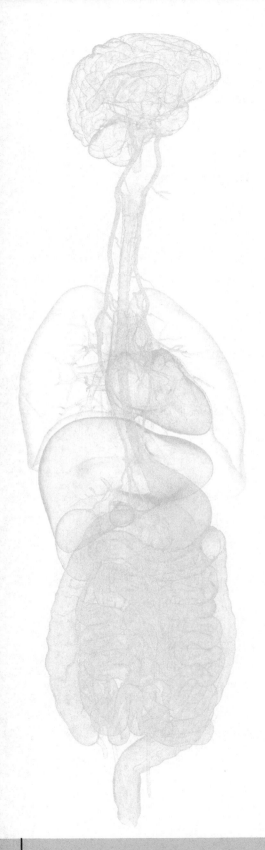

CHAPTER #8: VAGUS NERVE STIMULATION FOR ANXIETY

Anxiety is one of the best to work on when you start to become aware of the vagus nerve. Here are some of the exercises you can do:

Treatment of the Vagus Nerve with Acupuncture

Acupuncture has been applied for more than two millennia to treat a variety of ailments. As the name implies, acupuncture is a medical task that involves the application of fine needles in specific parts of the body, called acupoints or points.

Acupuncture originated in Asia and, according to acupuncturists, promotes the flow of Qi, the vital force that circulates through our body in the form of meridians. Acupuncture points are believed to be associated with pathophysiology, meaning that they reflect the state of internal organs and general conditions. Therefore, stimulating specific acupuncture points can also trigger the vagus nerve response and improve its tone.

Acupuncture stimulates acupuncture points or severely affected areas for muscle healing. On the other hand, distal acupuncture stimulation is used to treat diseases present in internal organs such as the vagus nerve.

Look for trained practitioners who use manual acupuncture, which involves sticking metal needles into the skin and manipulating it by turning it in one or two directions or lifting and pushing it.

According to practitioners, you can have a feeling that it extends to every corner of the body, which is considered a useful criterion for evaluating the effectiveness of acupuncture. Acupuncture has been reported to be effective in treating various diseases due to its ability to modulate inflammatory responses. This exercise cannot be done on your own; therefore, you could consider it so that you can look in your city where you do acupuncture and try it.

Abdominal Breathing

One of the main ways to stimulate healthy vagal function is with abdominal breathing that becomes slow and deep. You can learn to use it with breathing exercises to let go of stressful thoughts or pain. The human brain is going to process one thing at a time. If you focus on the rhythm of how you breathe, you won't focus on the stressor.

When you anticipate stress of any kind, many people tend to stop breathing and hold their breath. Doing this activates the fight/flight/frostbite response; it often increases the feeling of pain, stiffness, anxiety, or fear. If you want to do this type of breathing, inhale through your nose and exhale through your mouth:

1. Breathe fairly slowly (aim for six breaths per minute).

2. Take a deep breath that comes from your belly. While you take a breath, imagine expanding your abdomen and expanding your chest.

3. Exhalation is longer than inhalation. It is the exhalation that triggers the relaxation response.

Additional techniques for you to stimulate the vagus nerve include:

- **Rinsing vigorously with water or singing loudly:** this kick starts our vocal cords, which in turn stimulate the vagus nerve.
- **Foot massage:** making a light touch or a firm massage will help stimulate the vagus nerve.
- **Soak your face in cold water:** Soak at least 2/3 of your eyes, forehead, and cheeks in cold water. This activates the vagus nerve, slows down the heart rate, stimulates the intestine, and activates the immune system.
- **Eating fiber:** this helps in stimulating the vagus nerve of the brain, which slows bowel movements and makes us feel fuller after meals.
- **Laughter:** laughter lifts the mood, strengthens the immune system, and stimulates the vagus nerve.

We must not always allow stressful situations to have a negative impact on our bodies and mind. You can stimulate the vagus nerve to send a message to your body that it's time to relax and de-stress, which helps it improve long-term mood, pain management, well-being, and resilience.

Closed Exhalation

The Valsalva maneuver is a different breathing method, named after the Italian anatomist and surgeon Antonio Maria Valsalva. You'll start breathing normally. Then proceed to close your mouth, cover your nose and exhale gently for 15 to 20 seconds through the closed airway. The resulting chest pressure will stimulate the vagus nerve.

Apply Cold Water to the Body

You will put cold water in an icy shower, or you can splash cold water on your face for about 30 seconds to stimulate the vagus nerve. Put the lazy into action in this way and help in reducing its activity, putting it in balance.

Conscious Physical Activity

Mindfulness-based movement (MBM) has been shown to be effective in promoting recovery for many people, including cancer patients because they are derived from polyvagal theory. Physical activity that involves social engagement can help people safely move from activity-induced arousal to calmer states. Physical activity eliminates vagal inhibition and stimulates the sympathetic nervous system by increasing metabolic functions such as breathing. When the activity is social, the social engagement system has the opportunity to regulate the system and calm the body.

Vocalizations

Part of the vagus nerve is located near the vocal cords and inner ear. Humming, singing, and gargling causes the vocal cords and eardrum to begin to vibrate, directly stimulating the vagus nerve. Yoga lovers recommend chanting "om" or other mantras to experience this, but simply humming any song can have the same effect.

Reliving Pleasant Memories

Others are encouraged to remember times when they were happy or loved. These memories will stimulate the release of oxytocin, a feel-good hormone in the brain that serves to calm and relax people in stressful situations. Imagining spending time with close friends or family that evokes a sense of security can also help activate the vagus nerve and promote the social participation system. Maintaining these connections with others is an important way to ensure connection.

Playful Experiences

Pleasure is a natural state of being, essential in a serious world. While it may be difficult at first, people should strive to bring out their playful side to find areas in their lives that bring them more joy. This can be done with others, in the form of a board or football game, or alone, in a creative game or daydreaming. Participation in games can stimulate social participation responses. Even with video games, building a Lego, which activates the child's side you have.

Being in a Quiet and Relaxing Environment

When others perceive their environment as safe, the vagal motor pathway lowers heart rate and suppresses SNS responses. In addition, systems of social participation are related to physical fitness. The muscles that control gaze, expression, and hearing are related to visceral states that promote physical growth and recovery. Soft colors, beautiful artwork, and aromatherapy are effective ways to create a safe and relaxing environment.

Slows Down Exhalation Breaths

Lower vagal tone is associated with anxiety. A high vagal tone indicates that our bodies can quickly return to a calm state after an overexcited event.

Our heart rate becomes fast when we inhale and slows when we exhale. The greater the difference between inspiratory and expiratory heart rate, the greater the vagal tone. So, slow down your breathing when you exhale.

Then the exercise is that you take air through the nose and then you exhale it little by little, as much as you can, and your capacity allows, you will notice in a short time the change and relief in stress.

Immanuel Lerman said, "We still don't know whether or not deep breathing exercise can cause neuroplasticity," is a UC San Diego pain management physician and associate clinical professor, and "clearly more work is needed to definitively answer this question." But he also described it as "an interesting question" in the context of vagus nerve stimulation.

Lerman and his team are studying how stimulating the vagus nerve helps reduce pain perception; their work suggests the method could be used to lower chronic pain associated with PTSD. Vagus nerve stimulation involves the application of electrical impulses to the vagus nerve, either directly or through indirect non-invasive stimulation.

His lab and others are studying whether this stimulation, when used on a one-off basis, can help people with PTSD. Lerman's group is currently investigating whether daily vagus nerve stimulation for a week can improve anxiety responses associated with PTSD.

"... vagus nerve stimulation can reduce anxiety, increase alertness, and possibly improve cognition."

Lerman explained that fMRI studies showed that subjects treated with VNS then activated brainstem regions important for signaling norepinephrine, which is both a hormone and a neurotransmitter. This increase, he explained, can "increase arousal, attention and decrease reaction time," all of which can improve neuroplasticity.

But for now, the only mental condition for which VNS has FDA approval is a major depressive disorder. Up to 35% of people diagnosed with the disorder do not respond to conventional treatments. Vagus nerve stimulation was approved in 2005 to help people with treatment-resistant depression.

The polyvagal theory has good effects using the natural braking system you already have in your body. You can train or develop your parasympathetic nervous system to control and prevent panic and anxiety.

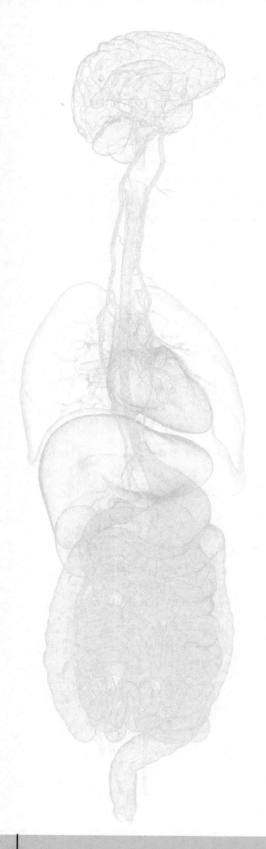

CHAPTER #9: VAGUS NERVE STIMULATION FOR ADDICTION

In a 2016 study done at the University of Texas at Dallas, rats were taught to manipulate a lever to hook cocaine, become addicted, and then stop taking the drug. Later, when the lever and associated signal were reintroduced, the mice exhibited intense drug craving and resurgent drug-seeking behavior.

However, rats treated with VNS engaged in these behaviors at a much lower rate. Some mice with VNS pressed 50% fewer levers than untreated mice. These results suggest that they experienced fewer cravings. VNS was found to alter brain plasticity to facilitate "extinction learning." This refers to a gradual decrease in the conditioned response. In addicted mice, VNS was able to create new rewarding behaviors.

VNS treatment can reinforce abstinence and ultimately steer patients away from drug-related behaviors, better protecting them from drug addiction. An undisclosed university is currently conducting a study in which they are testing the effects of VNS on people who have alcohol problems. More research is needed to determine the best way to implement VNS in addiction treatment, but the initial results promise much. It is hoped to learn more about VNS as a treatment for substance use disorders and addiction.

Instead of reducing symptoms in those currently struggling with substance abuse, VNS therapy "significantly" reduced the need to seek out and use these drugs. Since obsessive impulses and their triggers and cravings are such an important part of the problem, this is an important step in seeing real change in this area.

So, what does this new treatment really do for people and for those who work addictions and their cures? In the mice involved in the study, it caused "alterations in synaptic plasticity between the prefrontal cortex and the amygdala in laboratory mice addicted to cocaine." In short, the way it affects the brain is that it rewrites what drug exposure has already rewritten. Instead of falling victim to the dangerous temptations that were generated by the chemicals behind the substance, this new approach replaces them with "new rewarding behaviors." Since the vagus nerve as we know is long, it plays a very important role in the functioning of the brain, which is part of why this therapy is believed to be so effective.

Stimulating this nerve with a few electrical pulses helps the specialist reduce the desire for large nervous effects. In addition, they work to dismantle the link established between taking these substances and achieving a perceived reward, which almost exclusively explains the widespread use of drugs. Without a sense of reward worth pursuing, people are much less likely to use drugs, especially when they become aware of their dangers and consequences.

There is no doubt that more tests will be done to know in detail how much vagus nerve stimulation can help addicted people. The minds behind this are dedicated to working to apply the benefits to people with other problems, such as mental health disorders, and treating the symptoms of addiction. Now, we'll just have to wait and see how far these results go when human trials begin.

HPA Axis

When a person abstains from drugs or alcohol, their hypothalamic-pituitary-adrenal (HPA) axis, which is a key endocrine highway, also loses balance. This axis is made up of the hypothalamus, pituitary gland, and adrenal glands. The hypothalamus is responsible for the release of the hormone corticotropin, which travels through the pituitary gland and triggers the release of corticotropin. This hormone makes another trip to the adrenal glands, leading to the release of cortisol. This process forces the body to be on high alert, even if there are no threats of any kind nearby. Studies have found that these alterations in the stress response may also affect the risk of relapse in chronic drug users.

Exercise Helps Take Away That Fight-Or-Flight Feeling

In the process of recovering from addiction, LDS withdrawal treatment helps with medications such as beta blockers and antidepressants to ease anxiety, combined with hospitalization and care. While these treatments are good and necessary, exercise will also help as a specific clinical therapeutic intervention. During the recovery process, the entire PNS system is shut down and put into balance. The amygdala is the area of the brain that carries distress signals to the hypothalamus. Exercise increases serotonin and norepinephrine, which help with relaxation and calm the amygdala, which rebalances the HPA axis. Physical activity also increases the neurotransmitters GABA and brain-derived neurotrophic factor (BDNF), which are critical for lowering restlessness and stress. Exercise during recovery can lead to:

- **Reduced muscle tension:** exercise acts as a circuit breaker, resembling beta blockers, which disrupt the negative feedback loop from the body to the brain, increasing anxiety.

- **A different result:** anxiety kick-starts the sympathetic nervous system. But these same symptoms go hand in hand with aerobic exercise, and that's great. If people relate the physical symptoms of anxiety to something positive, which can have control, then the memory of fear goes in front of a healthy way.

Practicing yoga, tai chi, or any other activity of mind and body will help you restore the ideal balance between the sympathetic and parasympathetic nervous systems. In an investigation, it was found that Qigong, which I showed you at the beginning, had an important beneficial effect on the anxiety felt by people with addictions. Studies also show that this type of exercise helps with anxiety and depression compared to medications. Yoga can also help with chronic pain in people who use substances such as drugs or liquor and provide an alternative coping strategy. Studies have shown that exercise like yoga can rebalance the vagus nerve. However, many people don't understand how it happens to people with LDS: access to the mind-body connection.

The Vagus Nerve, Yoga, and the Mind-Body Connection

Based on the theory of Steven Porges, it is known that the ventral vagus or social commitment system has responsibility in situations without threat. It is like a brake that slows down our heart and other organs, which calms our system. Yoga activates the vagus nerve and branches that regulate the heart, abdomen viscera, face, and breathing. Nerves also communicate with the brain. Activating the vagus nerve while doing yoga helps regulate the sympathetic nervous system downwards. What saves people, especially those with trauma, gain self-efficacy while improving ANS regulation.

Mike Huggins, founder of the Transformation Yoga Project (TYP) and author of

Yoga for Recovery: A Practical Guide to Healing, understands the critical role of the vagus nerve, especially during recovery. TYP treats people affected by trauma, addiction, and incarceration through trauma-sensitive mindfulness that is based on yoga. There is a total link between trauma and substance abuse disorders. Incorporating trauma-informed approaches, such as yoga, into recovery helps people heal from trauma and stay in lifelong recovery. Hudgens explains how to use gentle yoga. This exercise activates the vagus nerve but also helps the recovering person know that they can choose their paths. Yoga activates the parasympathetic area and vagus nerve, which calms anxiety and stress.

Ways to Hack Your Brain to Help You with Addictions

There is no doubt that the vagus nerve can have a great impact on mental health and possesses the ability to improve it. I leave you a list of simple but effective tips to improve your mental health! Several of them we have done in other chapters, they are similar, but with the mindset of treating addiction.

Deep, Slow Breathing

When you breathe slowly, you can stimulate the vagus nerve. Instead of taking more than 10 breaths per minute like most people do automatically, try slowing down to around 6 breaths per minute.

Inhale and let your stomach expand while practicing mindful breathing. Then you exhale slowly and deeply.

This way of breathing will help you control stress and reduce anxiety, helping you gradually increase your sense of well-being.

Exposition to Cold

While exposure to cold may not always feel its best at first, it's a great way to activate the vagus nerve!

It could be that you stick your head in a sink full of cold water or force yourself to take an icy shower. In the process, you will surely stimulate your vagus nerve and improve your mental health.

Yoga and Meditation

Anyone who has experienced yoga and meditation can surely tell you that it helps to achieve a state of relaxation.

Yoga kick-starts GABA, a neurotransmitter that influences the brain to become calm. Meditation also increases vagal tone and positive mood, which helps you feel good about yourself.

Exercise

Physical health undoubtedly has an important aspect of mental health. Exercise is also a great way to stimulate the vagus nerve!

Regular exercise is a great way to get the boost you need and release plenty of endorphins in your body. The better you feel physically, the better you will feel mentally.

Relax the Back, Relax the Mind

They are light, elementary, and easy to perform exercises. For the first one we are going to do, you will need two mats (or a mat and a towel).

Follow this sequence:

1. You lie on the floor.

2. Put a reinforcement under your back that reaches your lower back. (Your chest should be higher than your legs.)

3. Put another cushion under your head.

4. Extend your arms.

5. Cross your legs so that your knees are at your sides, as shown in the image above.

6. You will notice some tension in your lower back and back area.

Now, inhale for 10 seconds, hold for 5 seconds, and exhale forcefully. Hold this position for 5 minutes.

Abdomen Up

This exercise also gives a lot of relaxation. You require a small bucket or stool or firm pads that allow us to raise the hip and abdominal area.

1. After you put the support under the area, bring your knees together.

2. Then extend your arms.

3. Now close your eyes and take a deep breath.

4. This position, in which our head is slightly lower than the body, will promote better circulation to the brain.

5. Have this position for 5 minutes and continue with the breathing routine: inhale for 10 seconds, hold for 5 seconds, and then exhale forcefully.

Balance with Your Legs Up

To perform the following exercises, you will need a mat and a cloth to cover your eyes and promote relaxation.

1. You stand in front of a wall and lie down so you can stretch your legs on it.

2. Place a pad under your back.

3. Again, your chest is going to be higher than your head.

4. Now cover your eyes with a cloth as you extend your arms.

5. You relax for 5 minutes, then repeat the previous breathing exercise (inhale-hold-exhale).

Probiotics

The health of your gut can have an immense impact on your well-being. The probiotics found in foods like yogurt help stimulate the vagus nerve, increase GABA, and reduce stress hormones. The vagus nerve is a powerful thing!

But one question can't be overlooked: If probiotics are so good, why don't we eat them every day? Or, in any case, when is the best time to do it?

First things first: Some people consume probiotics regularly. This is because certain foods are probiotics. The biggest example is:

- ☒ Sauerkraut

- ☒ Kefir

- ☒ Kimchi

- ☒ Kombucha

- ☒ Miso

- ☒ Tempeh

- ☒ Yogurt

Indeed, with the possible exception of yogurt, some of these are entirely exotic foods consumed by a few. That doesn't make it worthwhile, but it clearly shows that we can at least consider eating more of them. If we are not willing to eat these products, we can always consider taking probiotics in supplement form.

When to Take Them

Some health experts and popularizers recommend consuming probiotics at different times of the day. Some say it's best taken on an empty stomach, while others say it's best taken with a meal. Measuring the viability of gut bacteria after taking probiotics is very difficult. That's why only one study has looked at this.

The researchers found that certain bacteria, such as Saccharomyces boulardii, were not affected by food, while others, such as Lactobacillus and Bifidobacterium, survived better when taken 30 minutes before meals. The time is longer.

The main problem faced by the bacteria that make up probiotics is that our digestive tract is completely uninhabitable. Especially since they have to pass through our stomachs full of hydrochloric acid, which is capable of destroying the vast majority of bacteria (whether they cause diseases or are beneficial). That's why the vast majority of probiotic food supplements we can buy are tested to make sure the bacteria that make them up survive this journey.

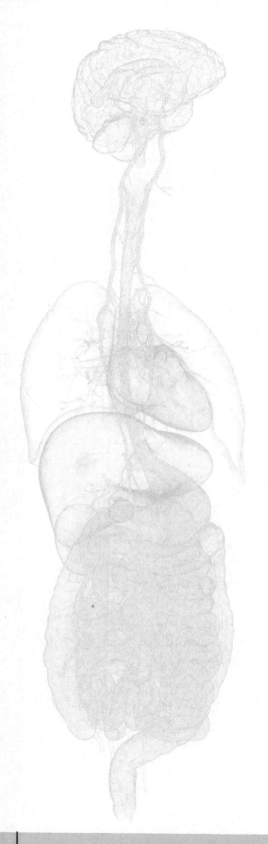

CHAPTER #10: VAGUS NERVE DIETARY FOODS (BREAKFAST)

The vagus nerve and food have a direct and decisive relationship with our health and well-being. On the one hand, we know that the former tells the brain to "stop eating" because we are full. In addition, it is important to know that this pulmonary-gastric nerve also regulates our emotions and has an impact on mental health.

In 1921, German physiologist and Nobel laureate Otto Loewi discovered that vagus nerve stimulation could regulate the heart rhythm and release a very specific fluid: he called it "Vagusstoff" (German: "diffuse matter"). This special "diffuse substance" is one of the most important neurotransmitters in our body: acetylcholine, which is the key to nerve impulses.

We have learned much more about this structure since then. It corresponds to the cranial nerve X, which is the nerve that emanates from the medulla oblongata and innervates the pharynx, larynx, trachea, esophagus, bronchi, heart, stomach, pancreas, liver, intestines... It is decisive because it is the main parasympathetic of the organism. The nerves and the functions they perform are diverse.

Now, scientists at Germany's Max Planck Institute have recently published a study that reveals something that amazes us. The vagus nerve has a direct and decisive relationship with feeding. It is the control center between the brain and the gut.

Emotions, Vagus Nerve, and Feeding

The vagus nerve is the most important part of the parasympathetic nervous system. This is because it consists of 80% afferent fibers and 20% efferent fibers. Thus, figures such as Prof. Wolfgang Langhans from ETH Zurich tell us that this structure is connected to our emotions as well as being connected to all our internal organs.

States such as stress or anxiety alter their normal functioning, which can affect the diet and intestinal flora. Research papers such as those from the University of Grenoble tell us how stress can upset the balance of the gastrointestinal tract and microbiota, and even contribute to gastrointestinal disorders such as irritable bowel syndrome.

Some of the foods you can consume to help with the vagus nerve are:

- **Fruits:** cherries, blueberries, blackberries, blackcurrants, grapes (preferably black and skinned), and berries.

- **Healthy fats:** cold-pressed virgin olive oil, flax oil, walnut oil, or sesame oil.

- **Nuts:** pine nuts, walnuts, almonds, sesame, chia seeds, or wheat germ, rich in fats of good biological quality and high-quality proteins.

- **Avocado:** the fat content reaches 15%, rich in oleic acid, palmitic acid, and linoleic acid, and of good quality. However, be careful as it is a high-calorie food.

- **Broccoli, kale, and cabbage:** they contain vitamin K, indoles, and isothiocyanates that have anti-inflammatory and detoxifying properties.

- **Papaya and tropical pineapple:** they contain proteases, such as papain and bromelain, which have anti-inflammatory properties. They are also fun in the form of nuts.

- **Green tea:** it contains polyphenols and catechins with antioxidant effects. Free of sugar and milk, this is a very healthy drink, especially compared to coffee with milk.

- **Shiitake and mushrooms in general:** some mushrooms are marketed as anti-inflammatory drugs. They are great for preventing low-grade inflammation. Shiitake mushrooms are probably the best known, but mushrooms and chantarelles also have anti-inflammatory properties.

- **Spices:** turmeric, ginger, cloves... You can add them to your rice and soups to give them an exotic and healthy flavor.

- **Tomato:** it is rich in lycopene, a powerful fat-soluble antioxidant. For this reason, cooking tomatoes, for example in the form of tomato sauce, increases the activity of lycopene. Tomato juice (natural, not bottled) is also anti-inflammatory.

- ☒ **Cacao:** cocoa flavanols protect endothelial cells (thin lining of arteries) from inflammation, which improves cardiovascular health. We are talking about pure cocoa, not milk chocolate. Chocolate with more than 70% cocoa contains quite a bit of flavanol, but the other 30% is also important. Avoid sweeteners and refined fats.

Foods That Cause Inflammation and Affect the Vagus Nerve

- ☒ **Sugar:** it's a power pump like no other nutrient. Its high caloric content makes it unsuitable for metabolic diseases and induces low-grade cellular inflammation. Avoid any product with added sugar.

- ☒ **Refined or very refined flours:** such as pastries, biscuits, white bread without crust, etc. They are foods with a very high glycemic index, more like sugar than unrefined carbohydrates. They provide a lot of energy and are therefore somewhat addictive.

- ☒ **Foods that contain trans fats (margarine):** they are processed fats, specifically pro-inflammatory fats. French fries, pastries, margarine, prepared sauces, pizza, snacks, coffee cream... They can all contain many of them.

- ☒ **Ice cream:** industrialists carry fats and other elements that have little effect on health. They are also pro-inflammatory.

- ☒ **Ultra-processed foods with added colors, flavorings, preservatives, or other additives:** fast food dishes, frozen meals, and processed meats were associated with increases in C-reactive protein, which in turn is associated with inflammatory processes.

- ☒ **Fried foods:** especially if you do not fry it yourself, we cannot guarantee the quality of the oil.

- ☒ **Alcohol, sausages, and dairy products:** if you eat them, they become inflamed.

Recommendations you can have in an anti-inflammatory breakfast:

- ☒ **Muesli:** make your granola by mixing ingredients such as cereal flakes (mainly oatmeal, but also granola), dried fruits (nuts), ground fruits (such as apples), apple juice, and some raisins or dried fruits. Soak the flakes in yogurt or juice first to soften them before adding the rest of the ingredients. It is an energizing, complete, and delicious breakfast that combines a variety of foods.

- ☒ **Fruit:** no breakfast should be without a piece. You can even eat fruit for breakfast. Pick them up from time to time, better if they are nearby.

- ☒ **Candied fruit:** cut into quarters a few apples or pears without skin or seeds. You can also mix them. Boil them for 15-20 minutes with a generous amount of cinnamon sticks, organic honey or syrup, lemon zest, and a little water. Add any dried fruit like papaya, pineapple, or blueberries to the compote. Serve immediately after cooking, or refrigerate for another day. Invent different models of preserves varying fruit, nuts, and sweet spices (cumin, fennel, cloves...).

- ☒ **Whole wheat toast with olive oil or avocado:** many people need starch for breakfast, and a toast or sandwich is an excellent solution. If you crave cookies, read the ingredients (preferably made from whole grains) and pay special attention to the type of fat that makes them. Avoid hydrogenated and preservatives, colorings, and flavorings.

- ☒ **Unsweetened cocoa drinks:** combine pure cocoa with a sweetener such as stevia or xylitol, stir well to avoid lumps, and add milk (such as rice or oatmeal) and a pinch of cinnamon if desired.

Vegetable Omelet

Eggs are one of the most nutritious foods you can find, and you can eat them whenever you want. They are rich in protein, vitamins, and minerals, such as selenium and vitamin B-12, and are low in calories. Putting some vegetables like spinach, peppers, and mushrooms in your omelet will increase the nutritional content and also add an incredible flavor to the eggs.

Oatmeal with Blackberries

Are you one of the many people who love carbs? The key is in the type of carbohydrates you choose. Avoid refined carbohydrates, such as bagels and muffins, and choose unrefined whole grain carbohydrates, such as oatmeal, which provide fiber, protein, and B vitamins. Add some blueberries for powerful antioxidant power.

Greek Yogurt with Fruits and Nuts

Think of this breakfast as if it were a dessert, and it is the most complete and healthy breakfast that exists. Greek yogurt offers you anti-inflammatory protein and probiotics to support better gut health. Fill your bowl with vitamin-rich fruits like antioxidant-rich blackberries and a variety of nuts like almonds and walnuts for healthy omega-3 fatty acids. Be careful when choosing yogurt, and choose plain yogurt that is much lower in sugar.

Peanut Butter with Vegetables or on a Toast

Few foods fill you up as quickly as this plate and also keep you full for hours. Add a tablespoon or two of peanut butter to vegetables and fruits like celery and apples, and you'll benefit from protein, fiber, vitamins, minerals, and a little sugar. The healthiest option is to choose one without added sugars.

Big Green Smoothie

1 cup almond milk, ½ frozen banana, 2 teaspoons chia seeds, 1 handful spinach, ½ cup pineapple, 1 tablespoon almond butter. Mix all the ingredients and place the coconut flakes, 3 chopped cashews, and cinnamon to cover.

Breakfast Bow

Base with blueberries, bananas, and 1 cup of almond milk. Top with strawberries, banana slices, cashews, chia seeds, coconut flakes, and cinnamon.

Rice Cake Sandwich

2 rice crackers, leafy greens, 1 teaspoon hummus, ¼ sliced avocado, sliced tomato, a pinch of kosher salt, pepper, and a few drops of balsamic vinegar.

Smoothie of Berries

1 cup frozen berries (strawberries, blueberries, raspberries, etc.), 2 tablespoons hemp seeds, 1 cup almond milk, 2 teaspoons chia seeds soaked in ½ cup water, and ½ banana. Mix all the ingredients, then add 2 tablespoons of quinoa or puffy

amaranth to cover.

Egg Toast

1 slice of rice bread (gluten-free), ¼ guacamole, 1 fried egg (better organic or free-range), a pinch of paprika, and slices of tomato or cherry tomato.

Green Juice

1 orange, 1 carrot, and spinach. Combine with water and put a packet of stevia.

Blueberries MIX

1 cup frozen blueberries, 1 teaspoon bee pollen, 1 cup water or coconut milk, ½ cup spinach, 1 tablespoon chia seeds, 1 tablespoon cocoa powder, and ½ banana. Mix all ingredients.

Vegan Pancakes

Soak in ¼ cup of water and 3 teaspoons of ground flaxseed for 20 minutes. Mix it with mashed bananas, a pinch of vanilla, and a teaspoon of baking soda. Put 1/2 cup of blueberries and make pancakes. If you don't want to mix the fruit, set it aside.

Oatmeal or Porridge

With vegetable milk, berries, banana, and flax seeds. What snacks can we have in the middle of the morning?

- ½ cup hummus with carrot sticks.

- A rice cracker topped with ¼ guacamole and toasted sesame seeds.

- Make a cup of pineapple and a handful of pumpkin seeds.

- 1 rice cake split in half with hummus and cherry tomatoes.

Breakfast Should Be as Healthy as Possible

A healthy breakfast can improve memory and thought processes. It has a positive effect on the body's anti-inflammatory processes. (Benefits such as disease prevention and relief of muscle pain and fatigue). A healthy breakfast increases the number of vitamins, minerals, proteins, and antioxidants our body can absorb. Many experts confirm that breakfast is the fundamental pillar to changing lifestyle and fighting inflammatory processes.

Avoid Certain Deceptively Healthy Foods

Those who have experience in nutrition advise reviewing products that "look" healthy. Some of these, like yogurt, contain extra sugar, which can end up contributing to inflammation.

Other products with which caution should be taken:

- ☒ Cereals

- ☒ Certain pre-made baked foods

- ☒ Granola

- ☒ White bread

Green Tea

A hot drink is very healthy. Several studies support its green tea binds to prevent diseases such as Alzheimer's and obesity. Green tea reduces inflammatory processes and increases antioxidant levels in the body.

Extra Virgin Olive Oil

It has a substance called "oleocanthal" that acts as an antioxidant and has effects similar to ibuprofen.

Oat

It has a high fiber content that serves to have good digestion. Depending on how it is consumed, it can aid in weight loss. But in turn, it can help increase muscle mass.

Avocado

One of the superfoods! It has magnesium, saturated fats, potassium, fiber, etc. Experts estimate that a slice of avocado can reduce the inflammatory process.

Broccoli, Cabbage, and Kale

They are foods that are rich in "sulforaphane," an antioxidant that protects against diseases such as cancer, reduces inflammatory processes, and minimizes heart disease.

Blue Fish

Unlimited source of omega-3 and proteins that protect against inflammation. Oily fish can protect people prone to heart disease or sugar problems. Research shows that salmon can help prevent inflammatory bowel disease.

Blackberries and Blueberries

They are fruits that contain "anthocyanins," which are antioxidants that slow down the inflammatory process and improve the immune system. They also help prevent heart disease.

Other Foods

Tomatoes, peppers, mushrooms, nuts, dark chocolate (over 70%), ginger, grapes, cloves, and fruits in general.

CHAPTER #11: VAGUS NERVE DIETARY FOODS (LUNCH)

Most diseases begin with a chronic inflammatory process caused by a poor diet and a sedentary lifestyle. This leads to the vagus nerve not being well stimulated and having health problems. More and more people are deciding to opt for a diet that avoids and prevents these processes. Following this diet is essential, so in this chapter, I show you some foods you can eat at lunch.

1.   Salad with Basil, Pine Nuts, and Tomatoes

Ingredients:

- 1 red onion
- 1 garlic clove
- 2 tbsp balsamic vinegar
- 1 oz peeled pine nuts
- 4 sprigs of basil
- 15 oz of tender shoot mixture
- 8 pear tomatoes
- Extra virgin olive oil
- Pepper
- Salt

Preparation:

1. Preheat the oven to 140°C/275°F. Wash and dry the basil, and peel the garlic. Crush basil and garlic with 2 tsp of oil.

2. Wash the tomatoes, dry them, and cut them in half lengthwise. Put them on a baking sheet, brush with balsamic basil oil, sprinkle, and place a few drops of vinegar. Add the pine nuts and bake for about 1 hour.

3. Peel the onion and cut it into feathers. Wash the salad sprouts, rinse them, and squeeze them.

4. Cover them with the remaining vinegar, oil, and salt and stir to soak them everywhere. Add the sprouts and onion and mix well.

5. It has 4 circles of dough in as many dishes as possible and fills them with the previous mixture. Put the tomatoes on top, carefully remove the rings and serve immediately over the salad. Add bell pepper to taste.

2. Zucchini and Mushroom Noodles with Tofu, Sautéed, and Cashews

Ingredients:

- 1 red onion
- 1 garlic clove
- 2 zucchinis
- 4 tbsp olive oil
- 15 oz shiitakes (or other mushrooms)
- 6-7 chive stalks
- Pepper and salt
- A handful of cashews

For the scrambled tofu:

- ☒ 1 tbsp turmeric

- ☒ 1 tbsp nutritional yeast

- ☒ 1 tbsp tamari

- ☒ ½ tsp smoked paprika

- ☒ 2 tbsp olive oil

- ☒ 9 oz firm tofu

- ☒ Sea salt or kala Namak salt

Preparation:

1. Take the tofu out of the package and wrap it with a cloth or kitchen paper, apply a weight (for example, a cutting board) on top, and let it dry thoroughly.

2. Meanwhile, wash the zucchini, remove the tip, and chop them in spirals with a spiralizer, or do it in Juliana and elongated with the help of a peeler.

3. Blanch what you left of the zucchini in boiling salt water for 2 minutes. Drain them and put them quickly in a bowl with very cold water. Drain them again and preserve them.

4. Peel the onion, which is in strips, and fry them in a large pan. Put 2 tbsp olive oil and leave it for about 8 to 10 minutes, low. Put what you have of zucchini, salt, and pepper, and sauté another little. Add half of the chopped chives.

5. To prepare the tofu, in a frying pan place the curcuma, tamari, paprika, yeast and then the tofu, which you are going to mix together and let it fry a little. This will accompany the final dish. When serving you can garnish with the shitakes.

3. Fennel and Zucchini Cream with Chip-Type Vegetables

Ingredients:

- 1 fennel bulb
- 4 cups of water or vegetable broth
- 1 potato
- 1 leek
- 2 large zucchinis
- Extra virgin olive oil
- Nutmeg, pepper, and salt

For chips:

- 1 beetroot
- ½ zucchini
- ½ cassava
- 2 carrots
- Soft olive oil
- Aromatic herbs or spices
- One of fresh rosemary or the same leaves of the fennel bulb to decorate

Preparation:

1. If you will prepare the chips yourself, make them before you start. You only need to chop the vegetables into very thin slices (2-3 mm), if you can with a mandolin or a vegetable peeler, put them in a large bowl and put olive oil and spices or aromatic herbs with which you want to season (for example, cumin, dill, curry, turmeric, paprika, garlic powder, rosemary, thyme...). It

combines well so that they impregnate. Then you can dehydrate them in the dehydrator or, if you do not have one, in the same oven: you put it at a temperature of 100-150°C/225-300°F and bake between 30 and 90 minutes, depending on the vegetable. You must open the oven from time to time so that the steam escapes or you leave it half open and put a wooden spoon through to prevent it from closing.

2. At the time you make the cream and the zucchini, wash them and cut them well, and leave them in pieces. If you want, you can peel them. Clean the fennel by removing the hardest base and chopping it into strips. Peel the potato.

3. Heat a little oil in a large saucepan and sauté the leek at a low candle, until transparent. You will often stir with a wooden spoon so that it does not burn.

4. Place the zucchini, fennel, and potato, which are poached a little, with the lid for two minutes, and cover it with water or vegetable broth. Salt and pepper to taste and let it cook for about 20 minutes until the vegetables look tender and the potato soft.

5. Remove the fennel, leek, zucchini, and potato preparation from the heat, crush them, and correct salt and pepper. Place a little nutmeg, distribute the vegetable chips on top, and decorate it with rosemary or fennel leaves.

4. Timbal Made with Peas, Tomato, Buckwheat, and Sprouts

Ingredients:

- ☒ 1 large very ripe tomato
- ☒ ½ oz radish sprouts
- ☒ 2 large carrots
- ☒ 7 oz peas
- ☒ 15 oz buckwheat

- ☒ 3 ½ cup water

- ☒ Extra virgin olive oil

- ☒ Turmeric

- ☒ Oregano

- ☒ Paprika

- ☒ Pepper

- ☒ Salt

Preparation:

1. Start by cooking the buckwheat and let it cool.

2. Peel a carrot and leave it chopped into small cubes. Put a pan on the fire and a little olive oil and cook the carrot with the pan covered. After about 15 minutes pass, or when it is tender, remove it and reserve. Continue with the process with the chopped tomato.

3. Cook peas in salted water for 7 minutes. Set aside 4 oz of peas and then decorate them, sautéed with a little olive oil and a touch of pepper.

4. Divide buckwheat into three equal parts. Crush the tomato a little, another with the carrot, and the last part with 4 oz peas. Put a splash of oil and a touch of pepper on everyone.

5. Season the following: Add some turmeric for the carrot puree; put paprika for the tomato; and put oregano for the pea. Integrate the spices well and set them aside.

6. Find a stainless-steel ring, put it on top of a plate, and place the first layer of the pea mixture, then another of carrot, and the third of tomato. Remove the hoop. Decorate it with reserved sautéed peas and sprouts.

5. Zucchini, Avocado, and Chickpea Hummus Served with Crudités

Ingredients:

- ☒ 2 zucchinis, chopped
- ☒ 9 oz chickpeas
- ☒ 2 tbsp nutritional yeast
- ☒ 1 lemon, its juice
- ☒ 2 cloves garlic sea salt (to taste)
- ☒ Water and olive oil, if needed
- ☒ 8 or 9 tbsp tahini (preferably raw sesame)
- ☒ 1 or 2 avocados

Preparation:

1. Combine all the ingredients in a blender, and do it until you have a texture that looks homogeneous. If it is too thick, you can add a little water and olive oil, until it is as you want.

2. Serve this hummus with sticks, which can make with celery, carrot, cucumber, or red pepper. Endive also goes very well with it.

6. Vegetable Sandwich and Hummus

Ingredients:

- ¼ avocado, mashed
- ¼ medium red bell pepper, sliced
- ¼ cup sliced cucumber
- ¼ cup grated carrot
- ½ cup mixed vegetable salad

- 2 slices whole wheat bread
- 3 tbsp hummus

Preparation:

1. Start by spreading one slice of bread with hummus and the other with avocado. Add vegetables, pepper, cucumber, and carrot as a filling for the sandwich. Chop it in half and serve.

7.   Black Bean and Quinoa Bowl

Ingredients:

- ¼ medium avocado, diced
- ¼ cup hummus
- ⅔ cup cooked quinoa
- ¾ cup canned black beans, rinsed
- 1 tbsp lime juice
- 2 tbsp chopped fresh cilantro
- 3 tbsp pico de gallo

Preparation:

1. Start by combining the beans and quinoa in a deep dish. Mix the hummus and lime juice in another small dish. Dilute with water until it is as you want it. Put the hummus dressing on top of the beans and quinoa. Top it with avocado, pico de gallo, and cilantro.

Tips:

So, prepare in advance: Assemble the bowl a day before if you want and reserve the dressing. If you do it before, to prevent the avocado from browning, put a little lemon juice after you cut it into cubes.

8.   Lemon Lentil Salad with Feta

Ingredients:

- ¼ tsp salt, or to taste
- ⅓ cup extra virgin olive oil
- ⅓ cup chopped fresh dill
- ⅓ cup lemon juice
- ½ cup finely chopped red onion
- 1 medium red bell pepper, seeded and diced (about 1 cup)
- 1 cup diced seedless cucumber
- 1 cup crumbled feta cheese (about 4 ounces)
- 2 tsp Dijon mustard
- 2 (15-oz) cans of lentils, rinsed, or 3 cups of cooked brown or green lentils
- Freshly ground pepper, to taste

Preparation:

1. Beat the lemon juice, mustard, dill, salt, and pepper in a large cup. Gradually beat it in oil. Put the lentils, pepper, feta cheese, cucumber, and onion. Proceed to stir it to cover.

9.   Salad with Tuna and Chickpea

Ingredients:

- ¼ tsp salt
- ¼ tsp ground pepper
- ½ cup crumbled feta cheese
- 1 tbsp unparalleled capers, rinsed and chopped
- 1 tbsp finely chopped shallot
- 1 (15 oz) can chickpeas with no added salt, rinsed
- 1 (6.7 oz) can tuna in oil, drained
- 1 cup thinly sliced English cucumber
- 1 cup cherry tomatoes halved
- 2 tbsp chopped fresh dill
- 2 tbsp lemon juice
- 3 tbsp extra virgin olive oil
- 3 cups baby spinach

Preparation:

1. Start by stirring the lemon juice, shallot, capers, salt, and pepper in a good-sized bowl. Let it sit for 5 minutes.

2. Mix the tuna, chickpeas, cucumber, tomatoes, feta cheese, and dill in a large bowl at that time.

3. Beat the oil with the lemon juice until it is fully incorporated. Pour about 5 tbsp of that dressing into the chickpea mixture. Mix to cover it.

4. Put the spinach in the dressing left in the big bowl. Stir to cover. Divide the spinach equally between 4 dishes. Top each plate with 1 ¼ cups of the chickpea mixture. Serve immediately.

CHAPTER #12: VAGUS NERVE DIETARY FOODS (DINNER)

Dinner cannot be exempt from healthy eating; these recipes contain ideal foods to stimulate the vagus nerve and keep it stable.

10. Sandwich Full of Cucumber and Avocado

Ingredients:

- ¼ cup thinly sliced red bell pepper
- ⅓ avocado, sliced
- ⅓ cup thinly sliced cucumber
- 2 tbsp ricotta cheese
- 2 tsp lemon juice
- 2 slices whole-wheat sandwich bread, lightly toasted
- 3 tbsp grated extra-strong cheddar cheese
- 4 tsp thinly sliced chives
- Pepper ground to taste

Preparation:

1. Start by stirring Cheddar, chives, lemon juice, ricotta, salt, and pepper in a small bowl. Place half of the mixture on each slice of toast. Now, put a slice with cucumber, pepper, and avocado, then cover it with the other slice, with the side to spread down.

11. Salad with Cucumber, Tomato, and White Beans

Ingredients:

- ¼ tsp salt

- ¼ tsp ground pepper
- ¼ cup extra virgin olive oil
- ½ cucumber, halved lengthwise and sliced (1 cup)
- ½ cup packaged fresh basil leaves
- 1 tbsp finely chopped shallot
- 1 tsp honey
- 1 (15 oz) can of low-sodium cannellini beans, rinsed
- 1 cup cherry tomatoes or grapes, halved
- 10 cups mixed vegetable salad
- 2 tsp Dijon mustard
- 3 tbsp red wine vinegar

Preparation:

1. Put basil, vinegar, oil, mustard, shallot, honey, salt, and pepper in a mini food processor. Process until it looks smooth. Take it to a big bowl. Put the vegetables, beans, tomatoes, and cucumber. Combine to cover.

12. Chickpea Puree in a Salad with Capers and Dill

Ingredients:

- ¼ tsp ground pepper
- ¼ cup chopped fresh dill
- ¼ cup vegan mayonnaise
- ⅓ cup finely chopped celery
- 1 chive, finely chopped
- 1 (15 oz) can low-sodium chickpeas, rinsed
- 2 tsp capers, chopped
- 2 tsp lemon juice or more to taste
- A stick of celery

Preparation:

1. Put the chickpeas on a kitchen towel. Fold it and gently rub the chickpeas, and remove the loose skins. Throw them away. Bring the chickpeas to a slightly large bowl. Crush the chickpeas. Put celery, dill, mayonnaise, capers, spring onion, lemon juice, and pepper. Stir until well covered.

13. Grain Bowls with Chopped Vegetables and Turmeric Dressing

Ingredients:

- 1 can (15.5 oz) chickpeas, rinsed
- 1 container (16 oz) of chopped vegetable mix
- ½ cup creamy turmeric salad dressing
- 2 packets (8 oz) of cooked quinoa

Preparation:

1. Start by preparing the quinoa as directed on the package. Bring to a shallow bowl to cool completely before you begin assembling the bowls.

2. Divide the vegetable mixture into 4 containers that have a lid. Cover each with a quarter of the quinoa and a quarter of the chickpeas. Then seal the containers and put them in the refrigerator for up to 4 days.

3. Carry 2 tbsp salad dressing in each of the 4 small containers with lids and leave it in the refrigerator for up to 4 days.

4. Combine each bowl with dressing before serving.

14. Quinoa Bowls of the Green Goddess with Shrimp and Arugula

Ingredients:

- ½ cup green goddess salad dressing
- ½ cup crumbled feta cheese
- 1 package (16 oz) large shrimp, cooked, peeled and deveined, frozen
- 1 packet (16 oz) of cooked frozen quinoa
- 1 package (7 oz) of baby arugula

Preparation:

1. Follow the microwave instructions on the package to prepare the quinoa (you require the two bags that are in the package). After you heat it, take the quinoa to a bowl not very deep so that it cools completely before you assemble the bowls.

2. Put 2 tbsp dressing in each of the 4 containers that have a lid and refrigerate for up to 4 days.

3. Divide the arugula into 4 individual containers (about 1 ¼ cups each). Top it each with ½ cup of quinoa and 2 tbsp feta cheese. Seal and refrigerate it for up to 4 days.

4. At dawn, before you put the packed lunch, put a quarter of the shrimp bag in a strainer and pass it through cold water until thawed, about 2 to 3 minutes. Put it in the meal preparation container. Season it with salad dressing just before serving.

15. Piquillo Peppers Stuffed With Prawns and Mushrooms

Ingredients:

- 1 onion
- 1 tbsp low-fat cream cheese
- 4 oz of mushrooms
- 11-12 piquillo peppers
- 7 oz of prawns (or prawns)
- Vegetable broth
- Skim milk
- Salt and pepper

Preparation:

1. Start by cutting the onion into small pieces and let them poach with the vegetable broth over low heat. Put a little salt.

2. When the onion softens, put the sliced mushrooms, and when they are almost done, put the prawns. If it is necessary, put a little broth so that it

does not stick and stir.

3. Put the spoonful of light cream cheese in the mixture and add salt and pepper. Stir often so that the cheese melts and looks like a thick cream so you can stuff the peppers. Remove from heat and let it temper.

4. Fill 8 piquillo peppers by placing them in a casserole or pan. Beat 2 to 3 peppers with some milk to make the sauce. You put it on top of the stuffed peppers and heat it all for 5 min over low heat and ready to serve.

Dinners with piquillo peppers can be very varied, follow these guidelines for low-calorie dishes, you can make a version of the classic piquillo pepper recipe, or add gulas and prawns, meat, or cod. In addition, in this case, add mushrooms to the recipe, so we get all the benefits offered by mushrooms: they provide hydration, are low in calories, rich in fiber, and contain antioxidants and vitamins B and D.

16. Chicken Breast a la Caprese

Ingredients:

- Oil jet
- Basil to taste
- A cup of chicken broth or vegetables
- 4 finite chicken breast fillets
- 4 slices of low-fat cheese or low-fat mozzarella
- Go out to taste
- 1 tomato

Preparation:

1. Place the chicken breasts on a kitchen board and cover them with plastic wrap. Set the blows with a mallet of flesh so that they are finite and soft. Put salt and pepper on both sides.

2. Put on top of each breast 1 slice of low-fat mozzarella, cheeses that do not fatten or inflame the body (and are healthier). Chop the tomato into very small cubes (you can peel it if you want it to have a finer consistency). Put in each breast the tomato and 1 or 2 basil leaves according to the size. Turn

on the oven to 180°F.

3. Make a roll with each breast, ensuring the tomato pieces do not escape. If necessary, close it with a toothpick as if it were a pin. Put it on a baking tray with a splash of broth and bathe the breasts.

4. Put it in the oven for 15 to 20 minutes, and when you see that the chicken was made and the cheese melted, voila! Put a splash of virgin olive oil, basil, and, if you have, a little Modena vinegar when serving.

17. **Stuffed Mushrooms**

Ingredients:

- 1 medium onion
- 1 egg
- 7 oz of York ham in taquitos
- 4 large mushrooms
- Oil, to taste
- Skimmed milk stream
- Go out to taste

Preparation:

1. Start by emptying the mushrooms and putting aside the filling of the rest of the mushrooms. Chop the filling very well into small cubes. Chop the onion and brown everything in the pan with a little oil and salt.

2. Cook the whole mushrooms seasoned before in a microwave dish for 3 minutes, or do it in Lékué. That you have the ham prepared in small pieces and turn on the oven at 180°F.

3. Beat the egg with a splash of milk and a pinch of salt, put it in the mixture of onion, ham, and the inside of the mushroom into pieces, and fill the mushrooms once you cook them in the microwave.

4. Put in the oven for 10 minutes and when you see the curdled egg, that's it.

18. Mini Zucchini Pizzas

Ingredients:

- 2 round zucchinis preferably
- 2 slices of low-fat cheese
- 4 slices of York ham
- Oregano, to taste
- Pepper and salt to taste
- Natural tomato with onion or without onion (optional)

Preparation:

1. Start by washing the zucchini and chop it into 1 cm thick slices.

2. Put on a griddle or frying pan on the stone so that the zucchinis are browned on both sides. Peppers to taste.

3. On the rack of the oven, put paper to avoid staining a lot, you put the zucchini. Place them in each one a little natural tomato that runs along the surface and put a little oregano.

4. Now to each one, put York ham and ¼ of a slice of low-fat cheese.

5. Turn on the oven to 180°F and put the zucchini until the cheese is golden. Serve hot.

As with piquillo peppers and mushrooms, zucchini can be prepared in 1,001 different ways, and the result will remain healthy and low in calories. Add an egg and basil omelet in a hearty salad, as if the noodles were instead of pasta.

19. Spinach Rolls

Ingredients:

- 1 bag of fresh spinach
- 4 eggs
- Pepper and salt to taste
- 4 to 6 slices of low-fat cheese

- 4 to 6 slices of ham or turkey breast

Preparation:

1. Start by chopping the raw spinach into pieces and put them in a bowl. Put the 4 previously beaten eggs, salt, and pepper. Mix well.

2. Preheat the oven to 180°F. Cover it with the oven tray with cooking paper. Put the mixture and spread it throughout the tray generating a layer. Place in the oven for a few minutes until it sets, and let it cool.

3. Once it is ready, place a layer of low-fat cheese slices, and cover it with another layer of ham or turkey. Wrap it, and you will have a roll the width of the baking tray. Chop into slices.

4. Put creativity and stuff in different ways, with cream cheese to spread, piquillo peppers, tuna, etc.

20. **Asparagus Cream with Crunchy Vegetable Bacon**

Ingredients:

- 1 lemon
- 1 potato monalisa
- 1 leek
- 2 bunches green asparagus
- 3 ¼ cup vegetable broth
- 8 slices bacon
- ¼ cup soy vegetable cream
- Olive oil, to taste
- Black pepper, to taste
- Go out to taste
- Black sesame, to taste

Preparation:

1. Chop the bacon into medium strips. Reserve.

2. Peel and chop the potato. Reserve.

3. Peel and remove the green part of the leek. Remove the white part and leave it sliced. Reserve.

4. Remove the inner part of the asparagus, wash them, and cut them into medium pieces. Reserve.

5. Heat olive oil in a pot and brown the bacon strips on both sides for one minute over medium heat. Cool and set aside.

6. Heat some olive oil in a pot and let the leek poach until it looks transparent.

7. Put the potato and asparagus. Let sauté for a couple of minutes, and add salt and pepper.

8. Put the vegetable broth and cream. Let everything cook over medium heat for a quarter of an hour.

9. Put the lemon zest, see if it is good salt and pepper, and crush with a food processor until you have a smooth and homogeneous cream. Reserve.

10. Serve the asparagus cream in a bowl and put a splash of extra virgin olive oil, black sesame, and crispy bacon.

21. **Spiced Mussels with Tomato**

Mussels have anti-inflammatory properties and are good for reducing and preventing cardiovascular diseases due to their high content of omega-3 fatty acids. One of its benefits is vitamin A, which serves to strengthen the immune system. They can be prepared in many ways: follow the classic recipe of Belgian mussels, curry, or simply steamed... Pending this delicious recipe of 4 mussels with tomato, which will undoubtedly enrich your dinner.

Ingredients:

- 1 garlic
- 1 shallot
- 1 tsp ground cinnamon
- 2 lbs. mussels
- 1 celery branch

- 2 tbsp extra virgin olive oil
- 2 bay leaves
- 3 tomatoes
- 2 oz of breadcrumbs
- Salt and pepper

Preparation:

1. Clean and wash the mussels. Peel and chop vegetables. Have a sauce with shallot, garlic, and celery. Then, put the bay leaf and mussels on it. Cover and, put on high heat, let them open.

2. Remove one of the valves from the mussels and put them on the plates covered with plastic wrap so that they do not get cold. Strain the juice they released in the cooking and set aside. Toast the breadcrumbs in the oven for a few minutes.

3. Wash the tomatoes and cut them in two. Steam for 10 minutes. Peel and crush them with a little (a deciliter, more or less) of the juice of the mussels you strained before. Add salt and pepper to taste and tsp ground cinnamon. Distribute the sauce through the mussels you left on the plates and sprinkle with the toasted breadcrumbs.

22. **Artichokes with Clams**

Artichokes are a natural food that burns calories effortlessly. In addition, given its high content of fiber, iron, folates, magnesium, and potassium, you cannot ignore it either. In addition to being one of the most recommended vegetables, it is also an easy ingredient to mix in dishes if the goal is to lose weight and combat flatulence (it is very diuretic).

Ingredients:

- 1 garlic
- 2 tsp white wine
- 1 lemon
- 1 leek
- 3 tbsp extra virgin olive oil

- 15 oz of clams
- 6 artichokes
- Salt and pepper

Preparation:

1. You need a little time to make this recipe, as clams should be put in salted water two hours before you start making them.

2. Peel the artichokes and leave only the heart, and chop in quarters. Reserve in cold water with lemon.

3. In a steaming saucepan, heat plenty of water. Place the drained artichokes on top of the rack when it boils and let them cook until tender. Then, drain them and reserve them covered so that they do not cool.

4. Finely julienne the garlic and leek and fry it with the oil. Put the drained clams, wine, and lids open. Then, put the artichokes, mix, and serve.

23. **Greek Omelet**

Ingredients:

- 1 tsp chopped fresh mint
- 1 clove of garlic, chopped
- 2 tbsp clarified butter
- 2 tsp EVOO
- 2 cups fresh spinach
- 3 large eggs
- 4 sliced green or black olives
- ½ tsp dried oregano
- ½ cup crumbled feta cheese
- ½ cup chopped cherry tomatoes
- ½ medium sliced green pepper
- Sea salt and black pepper to taste

Preparation:

1. Put in a pan 1 tbsp clarified butter, place the green pepper, and leave it

over medium-high heat for about 15 minutes. Now put the garlic and sauté one more minute. Then add the spinach and aromatic herbs until they are poached. Set aside afterward in a bowl.

2. Beat the eggs in a bowl and grease them again. Put a little salt and pepper on the egg mixture and when the pan has already heated, put everything on it, without letting the egg stick to the walls of the pan.

3. When the top is almost done, put the mixture of preserved vegetables, put on top of the tomatoes, feta cheese, olives, and aromatic herbs that you have left. Sprinkle with a little EVOO and fold the tortilla in two. When it is, slide it on a plate and serve.

24. Cold Coconut and Avocado Soup

Ingredients:

- 1 medium cucumber
- 1 cup coconut milk
- 2 large avocados
- 2 garlic cloves, crushed
- 3 cups vegetable broth
- EVOO
- ½ small yellow onion
- ½ cup lime juice

Preparation:

1. Place all ingredients in a blender glass (minus EVOO) and blend until there are no lumps.

2. Serve the soup cold and decorate it later with a splash of EVOO on top; you can put aromatic herbs and a little garlic focaccia or a little feta cheese.

CHAPTER #13: EIGHTEEN PRACTICAL STEPS TO STIMULATE NV NATIVELY

When you work on stimulating the vagus nerve, you're sending messages to your body and mind saying it's time to relax and let go of stress. Ultimately, this improves your life in many different ways, such as allowing you to sleep better, improving your overall mood, helping you manage pain, and improving overall resilience and well-being.

If you put yourself into fight or flight mode, you suddenly apply a lot of stress to your body. The body goes into a mode to flee the scene or fight whatever is in front of it. If this happens too often, the body begins to experience chronic stress, which causes the release of hormones such as cortisol. This constant release can eventually lead to health problems such as anxiety, mood swings, and indigestion.

Working the vagus nerve can help you counteract this response by helping to bring relaxation and helping you process the current situation. As it turns out, it's actually a big part of how our minds and bodies work!

What I will show you next will help you apply it from early in the morning until dusk and combine it with your daily activities, taking care to have the nerve always stimulated and in action.

Start Breathing Exercises in Bed

With one hand on your chest and the other on your belly, inhale deeply through your nose, making sure your diaphragm (not your chest) is filled with enough air to expand your lungs. The goal is to breathe slowly, 6 to 10 times per minute, for 10 minutes a day to experience an immediate drop in blood pressure and heart. It's something you can do every morning while you're done waking up.

Nadi Shodhana or "Alternating Breathing Through the Nostrils"

This is a yoga practitioner's best friend, as this breath is said to bring calm and balance, help the vagus nerve, and unify the left and right regions of the brain. From a comfortable meditation position, take your right thumb and put it into your right nostril, then inhale deeply through your left nostril. Cover your left nostril and exhale through your right nostril at the highest point of your inhalation. Continuing with this pattern, inhale through the right nostril, then close it with your right thumb and exhale through the left nostril.

Get Up Little by Little and Stretch

Now proceed to follow the breath and stretch the body.

1. Remove the blanket or sheet so that you have enough space and do not get tangled.
2. Start with bent legs: first, raise your knees and feet, then raise your knees in the air, lift your feet up and down, and turn your ankles in a circular motion.
3. Repeat similar movements with your arms, elbows, wrists, and hands.
4. Then, slowly sit on the bed. Slowly move your neck to the right and then to the left. Relax your shoulders and twist them. Try to feel how each part of your body prepares for the day.

Stretching when standing up:

1. Once standing, you can start a more complete stretching routine.
2. Stretch the neck: lean sideways, do not do strenuous exercises. You can help with your hands. Also, do it back and forth.
3. Stretch your legs: You choose the complexity of these stretches when you wake up. It can be as simple as doing a few squats or as complex as doing "butterflies" with your knees while sitting on the floor.
4. Stretch your back: You have to be especially careful with this part of the body because it is prone to injury. The idea is that you find an exercise that releases all the tension accumulated throughout the night.
5. Stretch your arms: the same thing happens with your legs, you decide!

Hum While Brushing and Gargling

1. To gargle, it can be with the same thing you brush or with mouthwash.
2. In small sips, bring the solution to the bottom of the throat, as much as possible. Gargle for about half a minute.
3. Spit. Repeat the same procedure as many times as you want
4. This way, you will stimulate the vagus nerve.

While Feeding, Meditate

1. Sit in front of your food and breathe several times deeply. Pay attention to color, shape, and texture. Does it look appetizing? Whatever your feelings about food, feel them.
2. Be aware of your intention to start eating. Slowly approach that food while watching the movement. You tell yourself what you're doing: "I'm going... Come... I do." By naming actions, it will be easier for you to remember your purpose: to pay attention. When you have the food in your hand, see that you are lifting it (and saying mentally): "Up... up... up."
3. Be careful with your hands when placing the sandwich in your mouth. When you put it in front of you, take a moment to inhale and smell it. What smell do you recognize? Did you notice the mayonnaise? How does your body react to smell? Are you drooling? Pay attention to how your body feels before you crave food.
4. When you take your first bite, feel as if your teeth are sinking into the bread. Where is the food in your mouth after you bite? How do you put your tongue on food to fit your teeth? Start chewing slowly. Have you noticed how your teeth feel? What smell did you detect? Tomato? Cheese? Where your arms are? Did you put it back on the table? If so, have you noticed movement?

Aim to Laugh All Day

Look to laugh whenever you can, whether watching a video you like in a break, talking to someone you know will make you laugh, laughing at what your children do, or sharing with your partner. Write down in the agenda five reasons to laugh and make it as serious as an office task and so funny that laughter comes from the soul.

Socialize

As much as you can, try to talk with others. Socializing helps the vagus nerve kick into action. At work, instead of sitting down to eat alone, you can, after meditating for a couple of minutes, talk to your partner about anything and when you leave too. If you work at home, socialize whenever you can with someone close to you.

Take a Walk Even If It's Inside the Office

If you have a schedule, you can get up now and then and take a walk. If possible, after lunch, go out for a walk a couple of blocks. Two laps of the block, 10 or 15 minutes of walking, will help you digest food and the vagus nerve work.

Do Slow-Breathing Exercises During the Day

As we saw the exercises throughout the book, set aside a moment to breathe slowly. You can do it while you work or while you think about something so your body will lower the revolution and feel calm and peaceful.

Hum While Working

Maybe you can combine, listen to music that you like and hum it. As you well know, humming and feeling the movement in the body will stimulate your vagus nerve.

At Noon Expose Yourself to the Cold

At noon you can go to the bathroom and wash your hands and then rinse your face with cold water. If you do not have it on hand, at least the one that is at the temperature in the sink.

Take a Sunset Yoga Class

These are the exercises you can do:

- You stand with your legs straight, your back straight, and your legs slightly apart.
- Now you have to rest your palms on your head with your elbows bent. If you find it complex, you can start by putting your hands in front of your chest.
- In this position, raise your right leg and rest the sole of your foot on the

opposite thigh.

- Hold this position for 30 seconds, then switch legs.

The Cobra

Another yoga pose that can be done at home is the one that has been nicknamed the "cobra" because of the way we pose to make it look a lot like the animal. This is a very simple asana too, to do it you have to follow these steps:

1. You lie face down on a mat with your legs straight out and together
2. At the same time, extend your arms, put your hands on the floor, and fully extend your torso back.
3. You should ensure your shoulders are relaxed, and your chin raised so that it is slightly up.
4. You have to hold this position for 30 seconds and rest for another 30 seconds.

Eagle Posture

Another yoga pose you can do at home is called Eagle Pose, and it's a little more complicated than the one I just told you about, but just as cool for connecting with your inner self. To do this, you have to do this step by step:

1. To do this pose, you have to stand with your legs slightly bent as if you were doing a squat.
2. You should bend your back slightly, without bending it or exerting force on the vertebrae.
3. In this position, you should bend your right leg over your left leg and try to bring your right ankle toward your left calf.
4. Hold this pose for 30 seconds, then switch legs.

Take a Cold Bath

Taking a cold shower is great to help you refresh and stimulate the vagus nerve, but that's not the only benefit it can do to us. Of course, the preference for water temperature is very particular, some people like to take a hot bath or soak in a hot bath. In this case, if your health allows it, take an ice water bath, or at least when you finish the warm shower, leave the cold water for a few seconds and get wet as much as you can.

Different Breathing Exercises

It's already night, it's time to try some breathing exercises:

Inflating a Balloon

It is quite simple to do and serves to improve your lung capacity and activate the vagus nerve. Take a balloon, take air through your nose, and inflate it. You can do it slowly, taking all the air out of your lungs, or do it quickly, holding short breaths. This practice strengthens the lungs and muscles involved in the breathing process, but it should only be done if we do not have any disease.

Open and Close Your Arms

For this exercise, open your arms and raise them to shoulder height, palms facing inwards. Then, take a hard breath through your nose while you try to relax your stomach. Hold your breath for three seconds, close your arms, and release through your mouth while pursing your lips. Inhale again while you open your arms and repeat.

Play Some Classical Music

Classical music can be a catalyst for good humor and has great potential to be a tool that allows us to improve our mood. Regularly listening to classical music can make us happier because of its harmony. It also induces a variety of sensations that affect the entire brain, which can help reduce pain and anxiety.

Several studies of people with mental illnesses such as Parkinson's, Alzheimer's, and other disorders that affect the human mind have concluded that the use of classical music as an adjunct or complement to therapy is positive. It is used as a tool in favor of the patient's willingness for other memory improvement exercises or as a technique to awaken neural connections.

Stress has become a feature of modern society, and most workers suffer from it; classical music can help them cope. Classical music helps relax muscles and lower blood pressure, and a study by the American Society of Hypertension showed that about 30 minutes of classical music a day can help lower blood pressure, which is essential for reducing stress.

Have Tea While Enjoying Mindfulness

This is a simple exercise to enjoy conscious tea, for this look for a brief guided meditation that will make you enjoy even more your cup of tea or infusion, preferably relaxing, such as chamomile.

1. Find a place where you can be calm, comfortable, and undisturbed. If possible, put your phone on silent. Cook the necessary utensils to make tea on a clean table. Place the crushed tea in a strainer and add water little by little. Watch the waterfall into the cup.

2. As the tea rests, keep in mind the position of your body. Extend your back, pull your shoulders back slightly, and try to be as relaxed as possible in a posture. Once placed, you will feel the sensations in your body and breathing.

3. I take two or three deep breaths and let the air start coming in and out as naturally as possible. Feel the air pass through your nostrils and watch the pauses between inhalations and exhalations. Try to relax with each exhalation. If thoughts or distractions arise, observe them and refocus your attention on the breath.

4. When the infusion is ready, remove the filter and observe the movements of your arm and hand until you remove the filter. Bring it closer and observe the soaked leaves, their appearance, color, and aroma. Try to do it as if you were looking at tea leaves for the first time.

5. Take the cup and look at its temperature; you may feel some areas warmer than others. Watch carefully how the tea moves, and the smoke it emits.

6. Come to it, feel its aroma, and discover its nuances. The smell of tea or any other sensation that may evoke a memory, a thought, or an image, become aware of it, connect with that sensation, and refocus your attention on the cup and hand.

7. I take a sip, noticing how the liquid rubs against the lips, temperature, humidity, and any other sensation in your lips and mouth when it comes into contact with the tea. You can repeat this several times before you start drinking.

8. Drink it again and notice how the tea goes down your throat, the heat, the humidity, the sound, and how the tea disappears again.

9. Savor each bite as if it were your first, paying attention to your body movements and taking your time. Stay present in the feeling.

10. This time, let your attention remain on the taste of the tea leaves. Appreciate the richness of the wine in the mouth, and watch how it expands, maybe you can feel it in different parts of the mouth, on the tongue. Notice how the flavor arises, how it is nuanced, and how it disappears. What does it feel like in your mouth when the liquid runs out?

11. Everyone appreciates these sensations, aromas, and nuances differently: it is the richness of each individual's attention span. We allow thoughts, images, and memories to arise, but again and again, we invite the mind to be with us.

12. Finally, put down the glass and look at the leaves again. Reflect on its origin and provenance. Imagine one day a plant with those leaves. How the tea tree grows thanks to the land where it was grown, the water and nutrients from the sun, and thanks to the attention of those who attended the tea tree and many others, who made it possible for you to taste this tea today. The connection between you and the tea you taste is huge. Recognize, value, and thank all your hard work, love, and dedication.

13. To get out of mindfulness moments, we can inhale and exhale more deeply and slowly. Start moving, imagining the environment, we resume our activities little by little.

Give a Massage or Ask for One

If you have a partner, you can ask him to give you a massage or do it yourself, if you have children, you can do a massage on the back, and feet, enjoying how the vagus nerve is activated by touch, as we saw chapters ago.

Do a Stretching and Relaxation Exercise

In any case, whenever you finish training, you should stretch. Follow these guidelines to stretch correctly:

1. Perform the stretch statically, maintaining the position without bounces or sudden movements.

2. When you stretch, take a deep breath and exhale air from your lungs, which will help your muscles stretch.

3. During stretching, "pull the muscle" until you feel light. Keep constant pressure at this point.

4. Hold the pose for 30 seconds. Studies have shown that it is this time that gives your muscles the most benefit. Range of motion improved after 6 weeks. After 30 seconds, the improvement doesn't matter.

Going to Bed Early Is a Good Habit to Follow

Sleep is another good habit that helps with the vagus nerve and with all health in general. The recommendation is that when starting this process, you start the steps to sleep better, going to bed no later than 11, if possible, at 10 and sleeping an average of 7 to 8 hours. Having a nice space and running sleep. This with the passage of days will improve your life in general and also the vagus nerve.

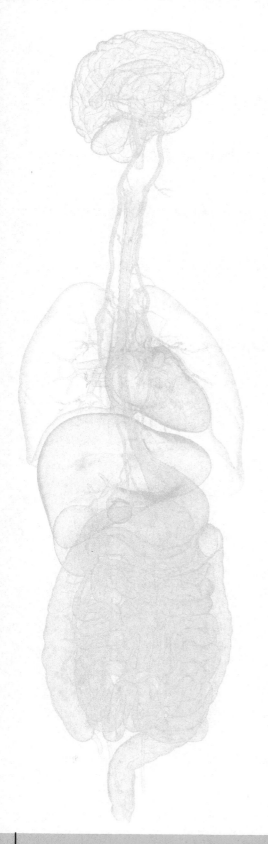

CHAPTER #14: 30-DAY MEAL PLAN

Below I share a series of meals for breakfast, lunch, and dinner, all made for you to enjoy and stimulate the vagus nerve.

Day 1

Breakfast

Muesli

Lunch

Salad with basil, pine nuts, and tomatoes

Dinner

Sandwich full of cucumber and avocado

Day 2

Breakfast

Fruit salad

Lunch

Zucchini and mushroom noodles with tofu, sautéed and cashews

Dinner

Salad with cucumber, tomato, and white beans

Day 3

Breakfast

Whole wheat toast with olive oil or avocado

Lunch

Fennel and zucchini cream with chip-type vegetables

Dinner

Chickpea puree in a salad with capers and dill

Day 4

Breakfast

Vegetable omelet

Lunch

Timbal made with peas, tomato, buckwheat, and sprouts

Dinner

Grain bowls with chopped vegetables and turmeric dressing

Day 5

Breakfast

Oatmeal with blackberries

Lunch

Zucchini, avocado, and chickpea hummus served with crudités

Dinner

Quinoa bowls of the green goddess with shrimp and arugula

Day 6

Breakfast

Greek yogurt with fruits and nuts

Lunch

Vegetable sandwich and hummus

Dinner

Piquillo peppers stuffed with prawns and mushrooms

Day 7

Breakfast

Peanut butter with vegetables or on a toast

Lunch

Black bean and quinoa bowl

Dinner

Chicken breast a la Caprese

Day 8

Breakfast

Big Green Smoothie

Lunch

Lemon lentil salad with feta

Dinner

Stuffed mushrooms

Day 9

Breakfast

Breakfast Bow

Lunch

Salad with tuna and chickpea

Dinner

Mini zucchini pizzas

Day 10

Breakfast

Rice cake sandwich

Lunch

Sautéed chickpeas with chicken and vegetables

Dinner

Spinach rolls

Day 11

Breakfast

Smoothie of berries

Lunch

Rice and lentil salad with avocado and tomato

Dinner

Asparagus cream with crunchy vegetable bacon

Day 12

Breakfast

Egg toast

Lunch

Chicken, quinoa, and bud salad

Dinner

Spiced mussels with tomato

Day 13

Breakfast

Green juice

Lunch

Pasta, cauliflower, and black olive salad

Dinner

Artichokes with clams

Day 14

Breakfast

Berries mix

Lunch

Lettuce tacos with lentils

Dinner

Greek omelet

Day 15

Breakfast

Vegan pancakes

Lunch

Warm salad of black beans and potato

Dinner

Cold coconut and avocado soup

Day 16

Breakfast

Oatmeal or porridge

Lunch

Green beans and sardines' salad

Dinner

Broccoli with quinoa

Day 17

Breakfast

Sweet kiwi omelet

Lunch

Whole grain couscous salad with red cabbage

Dinner

Chicken with vegetables with a papillote

Day 18

Breakfast

Kiwi glass with a granola base

Lunch

Pumpkin and oatmeal burgers

Dinner

Whole wheat toast with vegetables and goat cheese

Day 19

Breakfast

Berry smoothie

Lunch

Quick chicken and chickpea curry

Dinner

Vegetable tacos

Day 20

Breakfast

Apple with corn crumble

Lunch

Microwaved bonito cake

Dinner

Lentil salad and roasted vegetables

Day 21

Breakfast

Crown of berries with cottage cheese and honey

Lunch

Microwaved chicken breast with vegetables

Dinner

Mini salmon poke bowl

Day 22

Breakfast

Vanilla and hazelnut yogurt

Lunch

Cod in tomato, leek, and carrot sauce

Dinner

Spinach and mushroom muffins

Day 23

Breakfast

Banana and oatmeal pancakes

Lunch

Multicolored salad with sautéed salmon

Dinner

Zucchini carpaccio

Day 24

Breakfast

Chia seed pudding

Lunch

Turkey and avocado salad

Dinner

Sautéed vegetables with egg

Day 25

Breakfast

Applesauce with fresh cheese

Lunch

Cod and vegetable green curry

Dinner

Crispy salmon with potatoes and asparagus

Day 26

Breakfast

Pancakes with lemon sorbet

Lunch

Sautéed loin with carrots, peas, and peanut butter dressing

Dinner

Fake tortilla sandwich

Day 27

Breakfast

Smoothie with fruit skewers

Lunch

Cod with steamed potatoes in a microwave

Dinner

Tomato toast and mozzarella

Day 28

Breakfast

Portobello sandwich

Lunch

Sautéed chicken with paprika with pumpkin

Dinner

Stuffed white asparagus

Day 29

Breakfast

Almond cookies.

Lunch

Sweaty chicken

Dinner

Cabbage skewer with peanut sauce

Day 30

Breakfast

Coconut yogurt with pomegranate

Lunch

Bluefish with potatoes

Dinner

Baked salmon with yogurt sauce

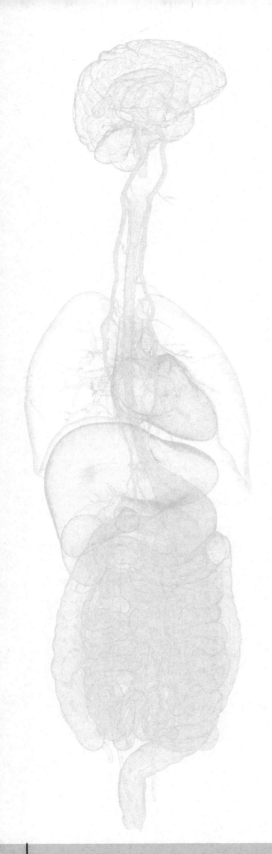

CONCLUSION

Controlling inflammation is one of the important functions of the vagus nerve, as we saw throughout the book. Inflammation is an important response that protects us from invaders like viruses or bacteria. When inflammation levels go unchecked and become chronic, the effects can lead to mental and physical disorders. That highway that runs through us and helps us control it is part of keeping us healthy, that lazy nerve that has nothing to be lazy about, must have a good run through our body to feel good overall.

Remember to keep in mind to reduce inflammation in the body through food. The state of brain fog may indicate inflammation in the brain, caused by a dysfunction of the blood-brain barrier and, therefore, a dysfunction of the intestinal wall or permeable intestine. As we saw throughout the book, all of this is a product of poor care of that nerve.

Some dietary choices can help reverse the inflammation and help improve brain, nerve, and even vagal function. They are summarized as:

- Eat real foods like high-quality fruits, vegetables, grains, or eggs.
- Don't overeat. If you eat slowly, you can enjoy every bite and feel more satiated by eating less.
- Mainly vegetables about 75%, such as fruits and vegetables, give priority to those that do not contain pesticides.
- Finally, do each of the exercises I shared throughout the book; you will soon notice the difference.

Our body is designed to live and survive without conscious thought. The vagus nerve is the conductor of the human symphony orchestra. This system is an evolutionary marvel. Simply put, it is part of the nervous system responsible for controlling unconsciously directed bodily functions: breathing, heartbeat, hormone synthesis, digestive processes, and so on.

As humans evolved, our ability to think consciously increased exponentially as survival systems became subconscious or self-regulating. It is left up to us to take care of ourselves and work to boost every part of our body and feel good.

Printed in Great Britain
by Amazon

23945868R00073